The Heart of Peak Performance

Emotional Mastery for High-Performing Men

to my brother,
my journey with high performers started with you

to high performers,
may you live the best of all you are

"Your task is not to seek for love, but merely to seek and find all the barriers within yourself that you have built against it."
—Rumi

Disclaimer

Throughout this book, you will find case studies and stories representing clients I have worked with. While identifying details have been significantly altered, the essence of their emotions, challenges, and processes remains true. These narratives provide an opportunity for you to see that you are not alone in your journey. The clients represented are men in their 30s to 50s, from various races and ethnicities, who are in charge of multi-million-dollar businesses.

CONTENTS

Introduction   1
   Who This Book Is For   2
   My Approach & Why I Wrote This Book   3
   Why This Book Matters   5
   What You Will Learn   6
   How to Use This Book   6

Part I: Inside the High Performer's Mind   9

1. Understanding the High-Performing Male   11
   What Is a High Performer?   12
   What Makes You Tick: Traits and Behaviors   13
   The Dark Side of Drive   22

2. The Roots of Emotional Disconnect   27
   Your Early Years (They Matter!)   28
   The Impact of Early Experiences on Brain Development   30
   Mirroring and Emotional Attunement   32
   The Power of Positive Interactions   33
   The Stories We Create   34
   How the Brain Processes and Stores Experiences   37
   Attachment Theory   42
   Beyond Childhood: Ongoing Life Events   48
   Breaking Cycles and Creating New Patterns   50

Part II: Neuro-Emotional Intelligence:
Your New Competitive Edge   53

3. The Neuroscience of Emotions and Decision-Making   55
   Neuro-Emotional Intelligence 101   55
   Key Brain Structures and Functions   56

How Your Brain Processes Information 63

Emotions and Decision-Making:
You're Less Rational Than You Think 66

Characteristics of the Male Brain 70

Neuroplasticity: The Brain's Capacity for Change 72

4. Mastering Emotional Intelligence 75

Why EQ Matters in Today's World 75

The High Performer's EQ Challenges 76

The Power of Self-Awareness 78

Emotional Intelligence and Influence 79

Leading from the Heart 83

Part III: Transforming Your Life (No-Nonsense Edition) 87

5. The Courage to Change 89

The Nature of Change 90

Taming the Ego 92

The Journey of Change: Stages and Challenges 94

Roadblocks to Look Out For 97

Hacks to Keep You On Track 99

The Case for Change 105

6. The Mind-Body Connection—Somatic Tools 109

Tool 1: The Mindful Pause 110

Tool 2: The Body Scan 112

Tool 3: Emotion Mapping 114

Tool 4: Feelings vs. Facts Check-In 115

Tool 5: Daily Meditation 116

Tool 6: Awe Practice 117

7. Becoming the Architect of Your Life 121

Rewriting Your Story 121

Connecting with Your Inner Child 124

Child's Truth Exercise   125

Witnessing and Integrating Emotions   127

SET UP: A Tool for Emotionally Intelligent Decision-Making   128

Journaling for Growth   130

Using the Past to Understand the Present   132

Self-Compassion and Healing   133

Positivity Practices   134

Living Authentically   136

Part IV: Leaning Into Love and Partnership   **143**

8. Understanding Relationship Dynamics   **145**

The LAB Triangle: Love, Agency, and Boundary   146

Intimacy Challenges for High Performers   149

Shared Responsibility: It's Not All on You   155

Vulnerability Unlocks Connection   159

Communication Basics   163

9. Building Healthy Intimacy   **171**

Strategies for Cultivating Committed Relationships   172

The L.O.V.E. Framework for Lasting Partnerships   176

Bridging the Sexual-Emotional Gap   180

Navigating Emotional Growth In Relationships   183

The Path to Secure Attachment   186

Balancing Freedom and Commitment   188

Conclusion   **193**

Additional Resources for Continued Growth   **197**

Acknowledgments   **199**

Works Cited   **201**

Introduction

Oscar, the CEO of a tech company he founded, appears to embody success. An immigrant whose family came to the U.S. with nothing, Oscar now lives a life of luxury, with multiple homes and extravagant vacations. But beneath these achievements lies a past filled with challenges and pain.

Oscar had a difficult upbringing. His father was occasionally abusive, and he even recalls one instance where he tried to pry his father off of his mother. After his parents split, Oscar took on the role of caretaker for his mom, but she often worked two jobs, leaving him alone most of the time. He felt like an outsider—disconnected and unable to relate to other kids. His unmet need for his mother's attention led him to believe that caring for others would only lead to pain.

Oscar didn't have his first girlfriend until college, and when they broke up—partly because her family didn't approve of his race—his belief that it wasn't safe to let people in was reinforced. When he first came to me, Oscar described himself as a high-performing CEO seeking to be held accountable and to get support with his leadership team. But as we worked together, deeper truths emerged. He opened up about his struggles with relationships, his reliance on alcohol and drugs to cope, and his fear of intimacy. He often lashed out at the women in his life, trying to dominate them, only to try to reconcile and understand his behaviors and emotions afterward. Though his actions were harmful, they clearly stemmed from unresolved trauma, not narcissism.

Through our work, Oscar began to understand how his childhood shaped his fears and unhealthy coping mechanisms. As he became more aware of his triggers and started rewriting the narratives that had kept him emotionally closed off, he grew more open to love and vulnerability. This led to significant improvements in both his personal relationships and his leadership. While his journey is still unfolding, Oscar is learning to embrace connection and love instead of fear and detachment.

Oscar's story is far from unique. Many high performers, despite living what looks like "the dream" from the outside, wrestle with similar obstacles. As a neuro-emotional performance coach, I work with clients who, like Oscar, have reached impressive professional heights yet feel chronically unfulfilled. They've got the accolades, the wealth, and influence, but behind the scenes, they grapple with isolation and strained relationships that leave them wanting more.

Who This Book Is For

This book is for high performers who, in spite of their success, feel an inner void. If you long for authentic connections and deeper emotional engagement, but feel trapped behind the armor of achievement, this book is your guide to embracing vulnerability and finding true fulfillment.

My Approach & Why I Wrote This Book

For over a decade, I've worked with high-performing men, including top-ranked professional athletes and CEOs of multinational companies, helping them navigate the complexities of leadership, relationships, and self-discovery. My unique background—combining psychology, human behavior, an MBA, and a strong foundation in neuroscience—allows me to help my clients bridge the gap between professional success and personal wellness.

My approach integrates cutting-edge neuroscience with practical insights and compassionate guidance, grounded in real-world experience and scientific research. It emphasizes a mind-body connection, ensuring that emotional, mental, and physical welfare work in harmony to foster true personal transformation. I've witnessed firsthand the profound impact of this work as I've seen high-performing men evolve from being successful in business but struggling in relationships to building meaningful lives where they lean into love—of self and others—with the same tenacity they apply to their professional endeavors. Additionally, my collaborations with institutions like Harvard and Wharton have not only expanded my reach but also enriched my expertise as a certified emotional intelligence practitioner, allowing me to bring even greater strategies to those I serve.

A recurring pattern emerges with my clients. Like clockwork, the initial meeting is always the same—they come to the meeting, hesitant yet curious, perhaps mandated by their board or driven by an inner knowing that something essential is missing. From the start, their guardedness is painfully evident.

When they start sharing, they might not be sure exactly what's wrong. They may feel disconnected from their team, struggle with trust, or simply sense that something is "off." Consciously or not, they seek external validation or material possessions to fill an inner void, masking the feeling that something is missing. Then there is the part of them that longs to share their darkest secrets—the things they've done, what they feel ashamed of, what hurts—but they feel there's no safe space to open up without judgment or rejection.

You may have seen the TV show, *Billions*, which featured the character Wendy Rhoades, a performance coach at a hedge fund who helped executives and traders work through mental and emotional blocks to perform at their peak. While her 5-minute pep talks solve everything on screen, real life is not that simple. Still, the show conveys the impact of emotions on decision-making and peak performance, and highlights the kind of elevated coaching high performers seek to gain a competitive advantage.

Time and again, the language used in executive coaching and leadership emphasizes concepts like driving, pushing, and relentless ambition. Knowing that our bodies have a visceral response to such language, I can't help but wonder if it's time for a different message, one that allows for the entirety of who we are to coexist. This book aims to provide that shift, offering a more compassionate and integrated approach to personal and professional development.

My passion and purpose is empowering growth-oriented high performers to live each moment fully, in all aspects of life, by understanding and overcoming the barriers that hold them back. This book extends that mission to help you spread your wings beyond professional success.

Why This Book Matters

As a high performer, you have immense potential to impact others. Your leadership and mentorship can shape industries, influence communities, and alter lives. But to truly harness your potential, you need to reconnect with your authentic self and lead from a place of emotional intelligence and openness. This book aims to bridge the gap between your professional achievements and personal well-being, offering insights and tools to enhance both areas of your life. My goal isn't to change you into someone you're not, but to inspire and empower you to fully step into the best version of yourself.

What happens to you personally affects you professionally, physically, and mentally. You can't disconnect from your emotions—they drive your thoughts and actions whether or not you choose to become consciously aware of them. Essentially, you are the architect of your own experience. You construct your emotional landscape and interpret others' emotions through a complex relationship between integrated systems. Your brain continuously predicts the world you encounter, striving for efficiency. It relies on signals from your body, interpretations, beliefs, personal references, and past events to guide your actions, ascribe meaning to your feelings and physical sensations, and assign value to people and events.

Understanding this system equips you to navigate your life in the moment. You'll learn to identify the contributing factors, recognize their effects on you, and redirect or redefine them to support peak performance. This knowledge allows you to cultivate a healthier perspective on what "optimal" means, moving beyond survival tendencies to achieve a more centered and enriching existence.

Through this work, you will discover how to create a more "balanced" life, recognizing that for you, that may differ from what it looks like for the average person. Additionally, you will improve your decision-making abilities, elevate your overall fulfillment, and align your inner being with your outward presence. While we look extensively at decisions related to intimacy, the principles apply universally to how you live, love, and lead.

What You Will Learn

In these pages, we will explore:

- The unique challenges faced by high-performing men, and why the traits that drive your professional success can hinder personal relationships
- How childhood experiences and attachment styles influence adult behavior and relationships
- The neuroscience behind your emotional responses and decision-making processes
- Practical tools to develop emotional intelligence and build deeper connections
- Strategies to overcome self-sabotage, embrace openness, and make choices aligned with your values
- A framework for redefining success to encompass both professional achievement and personal growth
- Methods to create true intimacy and stronger relationships

How to Use This Book

This book weaves together scientific insights, practical strategies, and reflective exercises designed to support your growth. Take your time with the concepts, engage fully with the exercises, and practice patience with yourself as you develop new skills and perspectives. Stay open to any insights that arise, and consider how they might inform your understanding or guide your next steps.

The information shared here is grounded in both scientific research and my professional experience. That said, science is constantly evolving, and new findings may refine or challenge what we currently understand—especially in dynamic fields like neuroscience.

While these insights can be incredibly valuable, I encourage you to trust your inner wisdom as well. The deepest truths often lie beyond facts. Pay attention to what resonates with you—what feels true, what brings peace, and what doesn't. Your spirit is a trustworthy guide.

Approach this journey with an open mind and heart. Your greatest capacity for change comes from within. You already possess everything you need for growth; this book is simply a tool to help you access it.

As you read on, keep this in mind: you don't have to take my word for it. Trust your own experience.

***

As a high performer, you've already mastered self-discipline, determination, and strategic thinking in your professional endeavors. Now, you have the opportunity to apply these strengths inward, towards your most important project yet: shaping a life that aligns with your deepest values and brings you true joy and meaning.

This process requires courage. It challenges you to face your fears, live by your values, build trust, and grow your resilience. Together, we'll work on cultivating these qualities so you can become not only a more effective leader but also a more authentic human being.

Whether you're here out of curiosity, necessity, or a longing for something more, my hope is that this book will serve as a roadmap for your journey towards self-discovery and growth. It's time to slow down, breathe, connect, and return to your true self. The world needs the best version of you—not just the successful exterior, but the whole, genuine, vulnerable you.

Are you ready to take on this challenge? To experience a new level of personal satisfaction that goes beyond material success? Then let's begin.

PART I

— — —

Inside the High Performer's Mind

CHAPTER ONE

UNDERSTANDING THE HIGH-PERFORMING MALE

"To confront a person in his shadow is to show him his own light."
—Carl Jung

We've laid the groundwork in our Introduction. Now it's time to get into the nitty-gritty of what makes you, well, you. As a high-performing male, you possess a unique set of traits, behaviors, and emotional propensities that set you apart. These characteristics have helped you to reach the pinnacle of success: the corner office, the seven-plus-figure salary, the accolades—they're all yours. Yet, as you stand at the top, surveying the empire you've built, why does it feel so ... empty?

If this resonates with you, you're not alone. Welcome to the world of the high-performing male, where professional triumphs often come at the cost of personal wellness. In this chapter, we'll dive deep into what makes you tick, exploring the unique traits that propel you to greatness—and the hidden costs that come with them.

— — —

What Is a High Performer?

Let's define what we mean by "high performer." It's a term that's often tossed around, but in the context of this book, we're referring to a specific and relatively small segment of the population.

A high performer is someone who:

- Consistently succeeds beyond the norm in multiple areas of life
- Quickly adapts to new challenges
- Maintains an extraordinary level of drive
- Has extremely high expectations and standards for themselves in all pursuits

Whether you're an elite executive closing a major business deal, an athlete pushing through a grueling training session, or a special operations member executing a high-stakes mission, your drive for excellence is innate. For high performers, there is no such thing as a "casual" pursuit—even a friendly game of table tennis becomes an opportunity to demonstrate mastery and go beyond comfortable limits. It's not external pressure that motivates you—it's an automatic, unconscious gear that kicks in whenever you face something (or someone) to conquer.

For you, excellence isn't just about your intelligence or capability—it's about your mindset, resilience, and sustained effort over time. You maintain focus and drive in the face of obstacles that would cause most to give up.

This book primarily speaks to high-performing men, drawing from my extensive experience with male clients who excel professionally yet struggle with vulnerability and connection. The insights shared here can benefit anyone who identifies as a high-performer. However,

I focus particularly on traditionally male traits—like the inclination to provide, protect, and fix—and their implications for performance and relationships.

Given your outward success, you might find yourself suppressing emotions and behaviors that seem at odds with your need to appear strong and in control. This pattern of emotional avoidance, while common, can limit your potential and impact your relationships, leadership, and overall wellness. Breaking free from these constraints is necessary for achieving deeper, more meaningful success.

As we explore the following attributes, keep in mind that you're not expected to check every box. These characteristics aren't meant to be a definitive checklist, but rather a framework for understanding the high-performing male mindset. Not every trait will resonate with you, and they certainly won't apply to every situation in your life. You're unique, after all—that's part of what's gotten you this far.

— — —

What Makes You Tick: Traits and Behaviors

1. **You seek accountability but struggle to find it.**
   You're at the top of the food chain, and the buck stops with you. Rarely does anyone hold you accountable for your behavior or challenge you directly. This creates a paradox where you desire accountability but lack trusted individuals willing to provide it.

2. **Failure drives rather than debilitates you.**
   Like everyone, you fear failure. But for you, this fear is fuel. Setbacks, especially in business, don't discourage you—they

motivate you to work harder. You transform potential defeat into powerful motivation, propelling yourself towards your goals. But when it comes to your personal life, your fear of failure can debilitate rather than drive you.

3. **Work is often a refuge.**

   You may use work as a place to hide from uncomfortable emotions or avoid dealing with personal issues. Professional success keeps you feeling accomplished and provides a "fix" of positive emotion without requiring deep emotional engagement.

4. **You feel driven to be seen as different or superior to others.**

   From an early age, your heightened sensitivity, complex thought processes, and keen awareness set you apart, shaping unique social dynamics. This early sense of "otherness" has persisted into adulthood.

5. **Your leadership style is blunt.**

   Your approach is direct, often characterized by sharp words and a stern demeanor, and can be perceived as harsh or insensitive by others. You excel at getting the job done, but your team may struggle to connect with you personally. This isn't due to a lack of empathy but rather your tendency to hide your softer side, viewing vulnerability as a weakness.

6. **You present with a high ego but often struggle with impostor syndrome.**

   What most people don't see is that beneath the confident exterior, you have deep-seated insecurities. Your ego serves as a protective shield.

7. **You're usually an entrepreneur.**

   If not an entrepreneur, you're likely the top dog—someone in an elite, decision-making role. You aren't someone who can be told what to do, partly because you struggle with social skills, and partly because your high IQ and rapid cognitive processing make it difficult to work for others without getting bored. You are fueled by high risk tolerance and an insatiable drive to succeed, which often leads you down an entrepreneurial route.

8. **You feel a great sense of responsibility for those who rely on you.**

   The weight of employee or team member livelihoods and their families depending on your success is a major motivator.

9. **People underestimate what it takes to be you.**

   Not everyone can perform at your level, and most can't imagine the pressures and challenges you face.

10. **You're highly analytical, prioritizing logic over emotion.**

    Your intense focus on your area of expertise reshapes your neural pathways, leading you to view the world through a lens of analytical thinking. This strong reliance on logic often downplays emotions, driving you to prioritize efficiency and excellence. As a result, you may find it challenging to adopt different mindsets in different situations, and this can diminish your capacity for empathy and awareness of how your actions impact others.

11. **You feel alone even when surrounded by others.**

    Your hesitation to trust and connect intimately with others leaves you feeling isolated. In addition, being who you are and doing what it takes to get to where you are is something few people can understand or relate to.

12. **Your resilience was often earned at a young age.**

It may have been shaped by life circumstances that required you to grow up quickly or by a challenging upbringing. This early need for resilience and self-sufficiency strengthened you to endure the challenges of the journey that got you where you are today.

13. **You push people away to avoid vulnerability.**

You view trust and vulnerability as putting all your eggs in one basket or giving someone too much control and power over you, which feels threatening. To protect yourself, you resist, fight back, or try to overpower others. Ironically, the people who could have this "control" over you are those you care about deeply. But instead of embracing that connection, you push against it. You distance yourself from the very people you long to be close to, preventing you from experiencing deep, meaningful relationships.

14. **You're often labeled as narcissistic.**

Though some high performers may exhibit narcissistic traits or even meet clinical criteria for narcissistic personality disorder, this is often a miscategorization. Your behaviors frequently stem from self-protective mechanisms rooted in past experiences or fears. In extreme cases, this can manifest as emotional manipulation—displaying whatever emotion seems necessary to achieve a goal, whether genuine or not. However, it's crucial to distinguish between actual narcissism and the intense drive that characterizes many high performers.

15. **Sexual performance is very important to you.**

    Sex allows you to feel something, to express yourself, to release emotions when you struggle to do so verbally.

16. **You're hypersensitive to perceived rejection.**

    When feeling emotionally threatened, you may lash out, shut down, or push people away more than the average person. This sensitivity often stems from a strong need for connection and security. Even though you can be affectionate and generous when feeling secure, perceived rejection may trigger defensiveness or intense anger, and the threshold for this trigger is much lower for you than for others. This emotional volatility may be more pronounced in personal relationships, even if you maintain composure in professional settings.

17. **Chaos is your baseline.**

    For you, chaos is often your mental and emotional baseline state, especially if you grew up in an environment filled with fear, stress, or instability. This has trained your brain to seek out a constant state of alertness, even when life seems "normal." Reducing feelings of anxiety can feel threatening, as lowering your guard makes you vulnerable. As a result, even when things are calm, your mind may unconsciously create challenges to produce that familiar state of tension.

18. **You're a perfectionist, driven by a need to control.**

    Your need to control is rooted in a desire for safety, which often presents as perfectionism. If you can control your environment, you can protect yourself. This can result in being overly critical—both of others and yourself.

19. **You believe that feeling your feelings will paralyze you.**

   You fear that if you allow yourself to fully experience emotions, you may get stuck and unable to move past them.

20. **You can lack follow-through on details.**

   Your big-picture focus, while valuable for leadership, can lead to overlooking routine tasks. This tendency may create blind spots in your personal life where details matter. Due to your very active mind, you might find it challenging to adhere to structured schedules and daily routines. You might have difficulty remembering important dates, managing household tasks, or attending to small but meaningful gestures in relationships. You typically need an assistant or "doer" to handle details that you can't be bothered with.

21. **You have a profound sense of pressure to keep "doing."**

   "When I'm not doing, I tell myself there's someone out there getting ahead of me, and I'm falling behind."
   "I always feel like there's someone on my tail." These are the mantras you live by, and they feel vividly real to you.

22. **Your mind is always active.**

   Your mind is constantly buzzing with ideas and energy, and high-speed thinking is your norm. You thrive on problem-solving and staying busy, often becoming restless when life gets too quiet. This drive propels you to achieve great things, but it also makes it difficult for you to relax and enjoy calm moments. You struggle to turn your mind off, especially when a complex problem or new idea takes hold, making it nearly impossible to disconnect from work or be fully present with loved ones.

23. **You like your alone time.**

In fact, you need it. Spending extensive amounts of time around others drains you, partly due to your limited tolerance for most people. This need for solitude can be misinterpreted by others as insensitivity or disinterest, perhaps straining relationships.

24. **You show different faces to the world and your inner circle.**

In public, you generally present your best self, carefully managing your image and interactions. However, with your inner circle, you may be less guarded, expecting them to accept you as you are, whenever you choose to engage. This contrast, combined with your sensitivity to rejection from close partners, can create challenges in your intimate relationships.

25. **You have a very small circle of trust.**

You allow very few people to get close to you. This guardedness often stems from past pain, perhaps from childhood experiences that left you feeling unsafe or unseen. To protect yourself, you've built emotional walls, making it challenging for others to connect with you deeply or for you to receive support. While this shields you from potential pain, it also creates difficulties in forming intimate relationships. You struggle with balancing your fear of vulnerability against the fundamental human need for connection and love.

26. **You protect yourself first, which can drive others away.**

When things get tough, you tend to protect yourself before comforting others, especially those closest to you, like family or partners. You might lash out or avoid being vulnerable to protect yourself. Such behavior can make your loved ones feel unsafe, causing them to pull away. As a result, you feel even less safe, prompting you to shield yourself further, and the cycle continues. This pattern can make it difficult for people to feel truly close to you, particularly during rough times.

27. **You're not one for celebrating successes.**

    As soon as a goal is within reach, you're already focused on the next challenge. Pausing to acknowledge your achievements feels unnecessary—what drives you is the momentum of continuously pushing forward. While recognition does feel good deep down, being at the top of the food chain—both at work and in your personal life—means success is often just expected of you. Genuine appreciation for your hard work is rare, leaving you without the acknowledgment you might quietly crave.

28. **Intimate relationships nourish you deeply when they're going well, but drain you intensely when they're not.**

    This one is true for most people, but the impact is disproportionate for you because you allow so few people to get close to you. When you *do* care, you care deeply, which amplifies their influence on you, both positively and negatively. Your armor comes down, leaving you more exposed, and managing those emotions takes a lot of energy. With so few close relationships, the ones you have carry an outsized emotional weight. Sometimes, another challenge is your struggle with a profound sense of inadequacy or low self-worth, though you won't admit it. This makes receiving love and positive appraisal from others a painful source of discomfort.

29. **You care more about the results than the journey.**

What matters to you is getting the task done, yesterday, often at the expense of "stopping to smell the roses." Your laser focus on driving results has likely been a key factor in your success, but it can also lead to a cycle of constant striving without satisfaction. You're always thinking about the next goal, rarely paying attention to how far you've come.

30. **You feel drawn to serve others.**

As you grow older, more successful, and advance in your career, you become deeply fed by helping others grow—particularly in areas where you are an expert. This can be true for many, but it's different for you. You're highly selective about who you let in emotionally, yet you're very sensitive beneath the surface. Serving others allows you to "feel, safely." Mentorship provides a way to connect, to expose yourself to the joy of helping someone, and feel seen, but with a level of detachment. This detachment shields you from potential hurt, especially in cases where you might perceive rejection.

How many of these characteristics do you identify with? Reading through them, perhaps you feel seen and understood in a way you rarely experience. This portrait is not meant to box you in or label you, but rather to create a starting point for deeper exploration and growth.

In the next chapter, we'll look at the roots of these patterns—how your early years shaped your approach to intimacy and connection. Understanding where these traits and behaviors come from is the first step in reconstructing them.

— — —

The Dark Side of Drive

For high-performers like you, success isn't just a goal; it's an imperative. When you set your mind to something, there simply isn't another option. You possess a next-level gear that others lack, allowing you to push beyond limits when others might falter. The concept of limitations doesn't exist in your mind; you persist until you achieve what you want, then immediately seek the next challenge.

However, this relentless ambition comes with a heavy cost. Many high-performing individuals, especially men in executive, elite-level, and entrepreneurial positions, may achieve great professional and financial success, yet feel a deep inner dissatisfaction. The stigma surrounding mental health issues, combined with the pressure to maintain a façade of unwavering strength and success, often prevents high performers from seeking the support they need. Studies show that CEOs and entrepreneurs experience depression at twice the rate of the general population, yet they have disproportionately low instances of admitting struggles or seeking help. Research on 400 high-achievers revealed that 75% had experienced troubled childhoods.[1]

Ultimately, your endless striving undermines personal relationships, emotional well-being, and self-reflection. The very traits that drive your professional success—single-minded focus, unyielding determination, and the ability to stretch beyond your limits—can also hinder your capacity for meaningful connections and self-awareness. While skills like competitiveness and strategic thinking propel your career, they generally do not foster inner fulfillment. This intense focus can lead to neglect of personal growth and emotional intelligence, making it challenging to build authentic bonds.

LONELY AT THE TOP

In a society that often equates financial worth with personal value, you may be seen as either a god or a devil. People view you as someone who has it all—you're successful, fit, attractive, well-dressed, well-traveled, and live a luxurious lifestyle. The world looks at you with envy, jealousy, and admiration. Yet what others don't see is your longing for vulnerability, connection, and the desire to lay down your armor and stop "fighting" ... often no one but yourself. Too frequently, people accept the mask you wear at face value, mistaking your wealth for self-worth, and allowing you to hide your more fragile self.

This intense ambition can lead to emotional disconnection from the negative consequences of your actions. As Tim Grover puts it in his book, *Relentless*, "Cleaners have a dark side, and a zone you can't enter. They get what they want, but they pay for it in solitude. Excellence is lonely. They never stop working, physically or mentally, because it gives them too much time to think about what they've had to endure and sacrifice to get to the top."[2]

THE PRISON OF CONTROL

Your need to control can drive people away, adding to the emotional distance you feel. As Michael Gerber explains in E-Myth: "Every strong entrepreneurial personality has an extraordinary need for control. Living as he does in the visionary world of the future, he needs control of people and events in the present so that he can concentrate on his dreams." The entrepreneur "creates a great deal of havoc around him," and often "outdistances others," further isolating himself in pursuit of his vision.[3] In addition, your desire for control isn't just about controlling others—it's also about controlling your own thoughts, emotions, and environment.

WHEN HAVING IT ALL FEELS EMPTY

Higher up the success ladder, the paradox deepens. Despite reaching heights that most can only dream of and having access to extravagant luxuries, you often feel unable to fully appreciate what you have. This is the core of the paradox: achieving "everything" yet not feeling whole.

Even in a crowd, you may feel profoundly alone. Despite your accomplishments and extensive network, you can feel isolated and disconnected from those around you. This sense of isolation is further exacerbated by the nature of your success.

While your drive has certainly propelled your professional achievements, the same success can obscure emotional or relational deficits. "Capitalism therapy" enables you to buy what you want, including temporary emotional connections (intimacy without commitment) or disengagement (activities that let you feel "something" without intense investment), preventing you from truly risking your heart. You might maintain dysfunctional relationships, knowing your partner stays for the material benefits, creating a feedback loop that justifies your unhealthy behaviors. This can lead to your social circle being filled with people drawn to your success instead of who you are as a person.

What it all comes down to is this: you have all the means, without the meaning. While your bank accounts may be full, your spirit often feels empty. This inability to fully enjoy experiences is a common complaint among high performers. The constant drive for more can rob you of the ability to appreciate what you have. You can indulge in extravagant adventures, yet miss the awe of experiencing them. This phenomenon isn't just a personal quirk—it's a symptom of a deeper challenge that plagues many high-performing individuals.

Take a moment to reflect on your professional achievements: When you look back at the path of your success and the potential opportunity cost, was it truly worth it?

Reflection Questions

1. Which high-performer trait(s) in this chapter do you identify with most strongly? How has it both helped and hindered you?

2. When was the last time you felt emotionally numb despite outward success?

3. How does your need for control restrict your relationships and personal fulfillment?

4. What one trait or behavior from this chapter most significantly impacts your quality of life?

CHAPTER TWO

THE ROOTS OF
EMOTIONAL DISCONNECT

"The wound is the place where the light enters you."
—Rumi

Now that we've painted a picture of who you are as a high-performer, let's explore how you got here. The traits, behaviors, and tendencies we discussed in the previous chapter didn't develop in a vacuum. They have deep roots in your early life experiences and the stories you've created to make sense of the world.

Let's dive into the origins of your emotional disconnect and consider how your formative years shaped your current reality, including your approach to intimacy and connection.

— — —

Your Early Years (They Matter!)

In my experience—100% of the time, without exception—high performers' struggles are rooted in childhood. Even when I've thought,
"Not this time. This person's challenges can't be tied to childhood,"
I've been proven wrong. Every. Single. Time. This holds true across all
races, ages, and ethnicities. In fact, for minorities, these issues are often
more pronounced, compounded by the isolation they may already feel
due to their background.

Now, I can almost hear some of you protesting, "My childhood
was fine! My parents were great." If that's your initial reaction, I invite
you to keep an open mind as we go further.

This isn't about assigning blame or labeling your childhood as
dysfunctional. While some parents may have caused serious harm,
most did the best they could with the knowledge and resources they
had. You're not broken, and there's nothing inherently wrong with you.
However, to truly understand who you are today, we must consider
your early years.

For high performers who claim to have few or no troubling
childhood memories, research suggests that this often stems from
growing up in an environment where emotional warmth was scarce or
inconsistent.[4] If you find yourself insisting that significant relationships
didn't affect you or that your recollections of family events are vague,
this could be a sign of emotional disconnection.

Take a moment to consider these questions about your childhood,
perhaps jotting down your thoughts:

- What was the energy like in your home? Was there tension?
  Laughter? Yelling? Silence?

- What kind of language did you grow up hearing? Was it critical or supportive?
- How were emotions treated? Were you told to "suck it up" or did someone say, "I'm sorry you're feeling sad … would you like to talk about it?"
- Did you have fun with your family through activities like game nights, vacations, or family dinners?
- Who did you turn to when you had a bad day at school or fought with friends? Did anyone at home notice or ask?
- What was your relationship like with your parents or primary caregivers? Loving? Critical? Distant?
- What stressors did your parents or primary caregivers face (e.g., immigration, financial strain, marital difficulties, emotional burdens)?
- Was there consistency in your childhood or instability (e.g., frequent school changes, moving often, finding new friends, an absent parent)?
- Did you ever feel rejected as a child by family, friends, teachers, or classmates?

There's no judgment on your answers to these questions. The goal is simply to explore the environment that constructed your early understanding of the world, relationships, and your own emotions.

As you reflect on your childhood, it's important to examine memories from the perspective of your child brain, not through the lens of your adult self. Your adult brain may now be able to rationalize your difficult early experiences and emotions, but it was your child brain that lived through those events and internalized them. Back then, you lacked the neural architecture to process painful situations in the same way your adult brain does now. Your child brain used these events to shape its fundamental understanding of the world and relationships.

Additionally, keep in mind that childhood "hurt" isn't always obvious or dramatic. It can take many forms—such as a parent's financial irresponsibility, infidelity, addiction, or anger issues. Even when not directed at you, these behaviors can disrupt the family environment and leave lasting emotional imprints.

— — —

The Impact of Early Experiences on Brain Development

Early experiences, particularly in your relationships with your primary caregivers, have an outsized influence on your brain's development and functioning because they occurred when you were highly impressionable. Children's early experiences form the foundation upon which all of the ones later in life are interpreted.

In *The Neuroscience of Psychotherapy: Healing the Social Brain*, Dr. Louis Cozolino explains:

"At birth, the more primitive structures of our brains responsible for social and emotional processing are highly developed, while the cortex develops slowly through the first decades of life. Much of our most important emotional and interpersonal learning occurs during our first few years when our primitive brains are in control. We mature into self-awareness having been programmed by early experience with sensory and emotional assumptions that we accept as truth."

This means that as a child, you were literally being introduced to the world, using interactions to understand what it means to feel safe, loved, seen, or rejected. This analysis was performed by a developing brain with limited capability in making sense of experiences. Your brain's primary objective is always to keep you safe and alive, and it achieves this through a combination of genetics, environment, and personal disposition.[5]

Dr. Cozolino further emphasizes:

"The result is that a great deal of learning takes place before we have the necessary cortical systems for explicit memory, problem solving, or perspective. Early experiences have a disproportionately powerful role in sculpting the networks of attachment and affect regulation due to the strength of learning during these sensitive periods. Just as positive experiences equip us with feelings of self-assurance and optimism, suboptimal bonding experiences become stored within implicit memory, carried into adulthood, and become woven into our adult relationships."[6]

The impact of childhood events on your adult brain is profound and far-reaching. Expressing feelings is an innate part of being human, so suppressing them requires significant effort and can be detrimental to your well-being. When you hold onto beliefs that intimacy and emotional connection cannot be trusted, these neural pathways strengthen over time.

— — —

Mirroring and Emotional Attunement

As children experience the world, they look to their caregivers to mirror their experiences. This mirroring allows them to feel seen and safe. When a child is scared, for example, they look to their parents for acknowledgment of that fear and reassurance that they're okay.

However, when mirroring and safety are absent (either because caregivers are not there, or because they respond with criticism, dismissal, or their own anxiety), the child may conclude: "The world can be scary, and I need people, but when it is, there might not be anyone there to protect me. It's not safe to depend on others or share my feelings."

Often, the person you longed for to soothe your hurt was the same one your brain perceived as the source of that hurt. This creates a challenging dichotomy: your brain simultaneously retreats from a perceived threat while yearning for safety from that very source. Your brain struggles to reconcile this conflict.

It becomes particularly challenging because children can sense their caregivers' emotions physiologically, even when not consciously aware of them. When mirroring is inconsistent, the brain, prioritizing survival, errs on the side of caution and decides to keep others at a distance.

Dan Siegel, in his book *Mindsight*, emphasizes the importance of caregiver attunement in building children's self-awareness and self-trust:

"When adults are in tune with a child, when they reflect back to the child an accurate picture of his internal world, he comes to sense his own mind with clarity."[7]

Siegel further explains:

"It wasn't until years later that I would come upon the research demonstrating how crucial it is to our development to have at least some relationships that are attuned, in which we feel we are held within another person's internal world, in their head and in their heart—relationships that help us thrive and give us resilience. And only later still did I learn how the neural networks around the heart and throughout the body are intimately interwoven with the resonance circuits in the brain—so that when we 'feel felt' by another it also helps us to develop the internal strength of self-regulation, to become focused, thoughtful, and resourceful. Being close to someone early in our lives gives us the clarity to know how we feel, and the ability to feel close to others."[8]

These early experiences create powerful imprints in the brain, shaping our understanding of safety, love, trust, and intimacy. They inform the stories we tell ourselves about who we are and how relationships work.

— — —

The Power of Positive Interactions

As a child grows, positive interactions with caregivers stimulate brain growth. Mutual eye gaze, physical touch, and emotional attunement all contribute to healthy neural development. In fact, research has identified over 900 genes that are differentially expressed based on the amount of maternal care a child receives.[9]

Optimal nurturing allows for:
- Increased neural plasticity
- Better emotional regulation

33

- Secure attachment
- Greater resilience and coping skills later in life

These enriching lessons allow you to form constructive definitions of fear, love, safety, and other critical concepts, enabling you to navigate emotional landscapes with greater certainty.

— — —

The Stories We Create

As we accumulate experiences, we either integrate them into our story coherently, or we separate ourselves from them by blocking, denying, or avoiding them. For many, especially high performers, this separation begins in childhood.

Growing up in an anxious or high-stress household—or in an environment lacking warmth and emotional security, where feelings are rarely discussed and vulnerability is seen as weakness—it becomes safer to distance yourself from these experiences rather than embracing or integrating them. This serves as a protective mechanism against the pain of unmet emotional needs.

In such challenging childhood environments, your brain creates the definitions it needs to navigate the reality it faces.

Consider this scenario:

You're eight years old. Both of your parents work long hours, so when you come home from school, you're usually alone. You tend to yourself, find your own food, and if you didn't come straight home, no one would know.

One day, after a rough time at school, there's no one to share your experience with. When your parents finally come home, exhausted from a long day of work, they aren't available physically or emotionally. They don't have the energy to give you the attention you need. Instead, you hear, "Did you finish your homework? Why aren't your chores done? You never listen!" By now, there's no point in trying to talk about your difficult day, so even if someone eventually asks how your day was, you simply say, "Fine" because you've already learned that your emotions won't be prioritized.

In moments like this, critical emotional needs go unmet. You feel sadness or fear but lack parental comfort to soothe those feelings. Without caring embraces, your brain has fewer opportunities to release calming chemicals like oxytocin, which help regulate stress. There's no safe space to process what you're going through, and you miss the vital lesson that experiencing tough emotions is normal and okay. Instead, you learn to keep your feelings to yourself.

You might create a story (based on your emotional, social, and neurological development at that age) that you don't deserve attention, that no one cares, or that your feelings don't matter. Children often internalize these experiences, blaming themselves as a way to make sense of the situation or feel a sense of control. All the while, your parents have no idea that this is the narrative you've formed.

As influential psychotherapist Virginia Satir said, "Every word, facial expression, gesture, or action on the part of a parent gives the child some message about self-worth. It is sad that so many parents don't realize what messages they are sending."[10] As you grow older, you carry the supportive or critical voices of your parents from your early years, balancing that internal dialogue with the language of your greater environment (partners, social groups, professional circles, etc.).

Although your adult brain may now comprehend the logic behind your parents' absence—they were busy working to provide for the family—the emotional impact from childhood often lingers. That eight-year-old part of you still carries the weight of unmet needs and the stories you created to make sense of your experiences.

Your present reality is influenced not just by your past, but also by the meanings you've attached to it. Consider the difference between believing no one cared about your emotions and having someone lovingly hold space for them. Carried throughout an individual's development, these contrasting experiences can create entirely different realities.

For many high-performers, common themes in their early stories include:
- It's not safe to depend on others.
- Showing emotion or vulnerability is a weakness.
- I must be strong/successful to protect myself.
- Letting people get too close will lead to hurt and rejection.

These narratives become deeply ingrained, often running in the background of your mind, shaping your behaviors and perceptions. And as unprocessed feelings accumulate over time, you compartmentalize them to avoid pain. While this coping mechanism can seem like a strength, it often leads to dismissing your emotional needs or feeling uncomfortable trusting others—without realizing these behaviors stem from early survival strategies. The result is a "false self " mask—a façade presented to the world—while your authentic self and true feelings remain hidden, pushed further and further down.

The good news is that the more emotionally aware you become, the less your unconscious stories control your life. As Anaïs Nin wisely said, "We don't see things as they are, we see them as we are." By uncovering the narratives that have shaped you and consciously reframing them, you can change how your past affects your present. This awareness gives you insight into your deeply held beliefs and emotional triggers, allowing you to see how past events continue to influence your responses. As you examine these stories, you begin to dismantle the walls you've built to protect yourself—walls that may have kept you safe but also isolated. Vulnerability, often a casualty of trauma, can be reclaimed as part of the path toward healing.

Understanding how these stories get lodged so deeply in our psyche requires a closer look at how your brain actually processes and stores experiences.

— — —

How the Brain Processes and Stores Experiences

Your Brain is a Database

Your brain acts as a high-tech database. It's constantly at work, processing and storing every experience you have. This isn't just about remembering your favorite sports team or where you left your keys—it's about creating a comprehensive guide to navigating life.

Whenever you encounter a new situation, your brain searches its database, drawing on your entire lifetime of experiences, paying special attention to events it considers important or potentially threatening. This is your brain's way of keeping you protected.

When you go to sleep at night, your brain is hard at work. It sifts through the day's events and decides which ones matter most. When it comes across memories of perceived threats or traumatic experiences, it doesn't just file them away. It tags them with emotional keywords such as "difficult," "hurt," "sad," or "unsafe." These tagged memories become your triggers, influencing how you react to future situations.

Here's where things get really interesting. Your brain isn't working alone—it's in constant communication with your body. The physical sensations become inextricably linked to the outcomes of events. Your body registers feelings and associates them with specific experiences.

This means that your brain's threat alert system isn't just looking for physical dangers. Both physical sensations and mental cues can trigger memories of past traumas or stressful experiences. For example, feeling tension in your shoulders during a big presentation might remind your body of past stress, thereby affecting your performance. Anything that resembles any aspect of a previously experienced threatening event can set off an internal alarm. This could be sights, sounds, smells, feelings, or tastes. It's like your brain has a vast network of tripwires, each connected to a different memory or experience. We'll talk more about the mind-body connection and tools for increasing body awareness in Chapter 6.

The brain then uses a feature similar to search engine optimization: the more a memory is "optimized" based on certain criteria (significance, how often it comes up, etc.), the more likely it is to appear at the top of the search results as your brain deciphers what's happening. A major contributor to this optimization is assuming worst-case scenarios when interpreting situations and creating "tags" to maximize survival.

It's important to understand that trauma is relative. What rocks one person's world might barely register for someone else, and what feels earth-shattering at eight years old might not carry the same weight at thirty-eight. The impact of trauma can vary not only between individuals, but also depending on the developmental stage at which it occurs.

When faced with an experience that resembles a threat, your brain defaults to learned behaviors to protect you. Over time, these responses become automatic. They form defenses that shield you from perceived harm by blocking out emotions and creating a barrier around your awareness. It's like your brain builds a fortress to keep you safe. You can't escape or outperform this process. It doesn't matter who you are or what you've achieved—this is simply how your brain works. It's not a flaw; it's a feature designed to keep you safe and functioning.

While these defenses can be protective in the short term, they may ultimately limit your ability to fully experience and reconcile emotions.

Your Brain is an Anticipation Machine

Beyond acting like a database, the brain also functions like an anticipation machine. It uses everything it knows—your beliefs, physical sensations, personal references, and memories—to try, in every moment, to predict what's going to happen next. This helps you navigate life more efficiently, but it can sometimes lead you astray.

Here's how it works: when you encounter a situation that reminds your brain of a past experience, especially a painful one, it quickly recalls that memory, predicts the outcome, and activates a coping response. In other words, once the brain has a sense of how a story will go, it fills in the blanks, often without regard for how big those blanks are. For example, if you were frequently criticized as a child, you might become defensive when your partner offers even mild feedback, misinterpreting their intentions based on your past hurts.

The brain also relies on creating associations, favoring consistency and predictability, which can lead to false causal links. As a result, emotions can kick in before a situation has even fully played out. Your past shapes your expectations and influences how you engage with the world. If these emotions are negative, they can cause you to misinterpret situations, miss out on opportunities, or create self-fulfilling prophecies.

It's important to understand that these associations are based on your subjective interpretations of events. You're not just passively recording what happens to you—you're actively creating meaning from your experiences. When you reinforce these patterns over time, they become more automatic and harder to notice consciously.

As psychologist Daniel Kahneman notes, "It is the consistency of the information that matters for a good story, not its completeness. Indeed, you will often find that knowing little makes it easier to fit everything you know into a coherent pattern."[11] This explains why we sometimes jump to conclusions, especially in emotional situations, even when we don't have all the facts.

It also explains why childhood plays such a significant role in our intimate relationships in adulthood. Your brain, always trying to conserve energy, relies on information it learned early on, and uses that to guide your decisions about trust and closeness. You associate certain emotions with past experiences, which then influence your beliefs and behaviors when you face similar situations in the future. For example, you might create a loop where closeness equates to pain, projecting this reality onto others who threaten to get close to you.

This is how your early relationships shape not only how your mind develops as a child, but also how you narrate your life as an adult. When you're operating on autopilot, you don't question your responses or examine your thoughts—you just accept them as truth. Your brain doesn't pause long enough to recognize, "Hey, this isn't exactly like that bad thing that happened before, so we're not in the same danger." Consequently, this quick reaction doesn't allow for a more thoughtful assessment of the current situation.

Though this system is efficient, it can also lead to erroneous predictions and jumping to conclusions, especially in emotional situations. High performers might be particularly prone to these misjudgments due to their rapid processing, lack of patience, and strong defense mechanisms from past experiences.

As spiritual teacher Eckhart Tolle suggests, it's helpful not to take your thoughts too seriously. Your reactions stem from how your mind interprets situations, not the circumstances themselves. "The thinking mind is a useful and powerful tool, but it's also very limiting when it takes over your life completely, when you don't realize that it is only a small aspect of the consciousness that you are."[12] Your brain's predictions are just one way of seeing things, not the absolute truth.

Fortunately, once you understand how your predictive brain works, you can start to work with it instead of being controlled by it. You can learn to pause and question those automatic predictions. Are they really accurate? Or are they based on old experiences that might not apply anymore? This awareness empowers you to make more conscious choices, handle your emotions better, and break free from old habits that aren't serving you well.

— — —

Attachment Theory

Now that we've explored the significance of early experiences, let's delve into a framework that helps us understand how they impact our approach to relationships: Attachment Theory.

Attachment Theory, developed by John Bowlby and expanded by Mary Ainsworth, posits that humans are born with a need to form a close emotional bond with a caregiver. This bond protects us from potential harm when we're vulnerable and regulates our emotions following threatening events. The nature of this early attachment profoundly influences our approach to relationships throughout our lives.[13]

A child's attachment style forms based on the parent's reaction to the child's expression of need and whether the child learns they can consistently count on that parent's presence and attentiveness.

Researchers have identified three main attachment patterns in children, which often persist into adulthood:

1. **Secure attachment**: Securely attached individuals are comfortable with intimacy and are able to depend on others while maintaining their autonomy. They tend to have trusting, lasting relationships and high self-esteem.

2. **Anxious attachment**: Anxious adults often worry about their relationships, fear abandonment, and require frequent

reassurance. They may become overly dependent or demanding in their quest for closeness.

3. **Avoidant attachment**: Avoidant adults are uncomfortable with intimacy and fear depending on others. They tend to be emotionally distant in relationships and highly value their independence.[14]

The majority of high-performing men I work with exhibit an avoidant attachment style, finding it difficult to trust others or let them in, despite a universal need for connection. As a result, emotions may be suppressed, and deep connections are avoided. They often come to believe that closeness is a greater threat than the pain of disconnection.

As these attachment styles take shape during childhood, they become a blueprint for how we navigate our closest relationships in adulthood. In romantic partnerships, attachment style plays a pivotal role in determining the quality and depth of a bond. In fact, research consistently shows that secure attachment is the best predictor of happiness in relationships.

Key characteristics of secure attachment in romantic relationships include:

- Emotional safety, allowing you to feel secure in loving and being loved in return
- A deep, visceral level of attunement with your partner
- Certainty that your partner believes in you, supports you, and prioritizes the partnership

When these conditions are met, a romantic relationship becomes a space for mutual growth and trust, rather than a source of fear or uncertainty.

A REAL-LIFE SCENARIO

To illustrate how avoidant attachment patterns play out in relationships, consider this common scenario:

You meet a woman you like. You're charming, successful, and intelligent. Initially, you present your "external self "—the polished version you show the world. There's chemistry, and you enjoy each other's company. This feels good because you've kept your defenses in place. You don't allow yourself to get too close, maybe even keeping other romantic options open to ensure you don't have all your eggs in one basket, and an escape route is always in place.

As you spend more time together, you become closer—not in the sense that you allow her in more, but you find yourself more affected by her. Being close feels nice, and part of you longs for the safety and partnership she represents—the brain's natural desire for attachment. Your brain says, "Here's a potential for us to feel safe, to have someone who can be our anchor and our rock," as it is programmed to seek that. But your embedded beliefs quickly jump in and say "Not so fast," reminding you not to depend on others.

When the relationship reaches a certain level of intimacy, your defenses get triggered. For you, the threat of someone getting close causes dysregulation much more quickly than for most people. Suddenly, you feel threatened by her desire for closeness. So, you push away. You are strong and independent. You don't need anyone. She just wants to lock you down and is trying to get closer than you are comfortable with (or at least this is what you tell yourself).

You start to view her gestures negatively, focusing on potential threats to your independence. The stronger your emotions about these perceived threats, the more you look to validate them logically with supporting evidence. And the more stressed you feel, the more you respond to her negatively, fixating on detecting dangers. This feeds your pessimistic views of the relationship. What emerges is a push-pull dynamic: you withdraw, then you feel a void and miss her, so you re-engage, only to feel overwhelmed and pull away again.

This cycle is exhausting and confusing for both parties. You might blame her for being "too needy" or "moving too fast," rather than recognizing your internal struggle with intimacy. And she, likely having an anxious attachment style, reacts strongly to your inconsistency and the resulting sense of loss, rejection, and instability. Your reactive state compromises your ability to interpret her words and actions clearly; you view everything from the lens of "she's a threat." This is not love—it's an unhealthy dynamic riddled with anxiety, insecurity, and obsessiveness that triggers acting out and shutting down. It often leads to ending relationships prematurely, suppressing feelings, and quickly moving on to the next woman—perpetuating the cycle.

There is a high price to pay for all of this. The struggle of constantly suppressing your attachment needs while longing to feel seen and connected is overwhelming. It's like you're drowning, occasionally breaching the surface for just enough air to keep you alive, only to sink back down below a surface that's always just out of your reach.

Maintaining this "representative self" robs you of the ability to be your authentic self, a critical factor in our well-being and relationship satisfaction. Operating behind these walls may feel safer, allowing you to act with greater self-interest, but it only prolongs your sense of aloneness.

How Your Parents Were Parented

Your parents' own histories play a critical role in shaping your attachment style. Like you, your parents were once children, and their experiences with their own parents laid the foundation for the adults they became. This intergenerational transmission of attachment is an important aspect of understanding your emotional development, creating a kind of emotional inheritance.

Imagine a parent who grew up in a home lacking emotional warmth. How could they learn to offer that warmth to you? If your parents struggled with emotion regulation or carried unresolved trauma, it would have affected their ability to provide consistent attunement and emotional safety. External factors like financial hardship, cultural displacement, or health issues could also have limited their emotional availability.

This doesn't mean your parents were "bad" or didn't love you. It simply acknowledges a basic truth: we can only give what we've received and learned ourselves.

Understanding this can shed light on your own emotional development. It can also help you feel more compassionate towards both your parents and yourself, empowering you to modify these behaviors. Though your life certainly has individual variables that were absent in your parents' lives, the core emotional tendencies often persist unless consciously addressed.[15]

Breaking this cycle isn't easy. Many of us, even those who regularly engage in self-reflection, can find it difficult to honestly assess our parents' emotional shortcomings. Even when we're aware of our childhood struggles, we might unconsciously repeat the same patterns with our own children.

The encouraging thing is it only takes one person to initiate change. By developing awareness of how your childhood affected you and doing the work to heal and grow, you can rewrite your story and create a new emotional legacy for yourself and future generations.

THE SIGNIFICANCE OF ATTACHMENT

Our brains are fundamentally wired to seek connection, a need that remains constant throughout our lives. When this need is met, we feel calm and secure. When it's not met, we may react with intense emotions—anger, anxiety, or withdrawal—all in an effort to re-establish that vital connection.

In their book, *Attached*, Dr. Amir Levine and Rachel Heller explain how this need begins in the womb and stays with us until death. They describe a dedicated biological mechanism in our brains specifically designed to create and regulate our bonds with important people in our lives—parents, children, and romantic partners. This makes evolutionary sense: in prehistoric times, staying close to others wasn't just about emotional comfort—it was a matter of life or death.[16]

This attachment-seeking behavior is deeply rooted in our survival instincts. When your brain fires up to seek connection and that need is met, the fire cools and you return to calm. But if connection is missing, the fire rages, triggering your nervous system and creating a physiological response. You might find yourself lashing out in anger, freezing up, or withdrawing in shame. Inside, you're often caught between two competing instincts: the urge to protect yourself by keeping others at a distance, and the fundamental need to connect.

This dynamic is especially powerful in childhood. For a young child, maintaining acceptance from their "tribe" (parents) is paramount, and leaving isn't an option. The instinct to bond with parents is so strong that it persists regardless of circumstances. Children often internalize blame ("I am bad") rather than attributing fault to their caregivers, as this feels safer for survival.

Understanding our biological imperative for connection helps explain why attachment dynamics can turn our world upside down—or right-side up. Our thoughts and behaviors are driven by this inescapable wiring that remains with us throughout our lives. However, attachment theory is not the be-all and end-all. We're complex beings who can't be reduced to a single label. Your attachment style doesn't define you—it's simply one lens through which to understand your relationships. At its core, attachment theory speaks to our universal human desire for love, safety, belonging, and being seen. While it can explain certain behaviors, it doesn't excuse them or absolve you of responsibility for your actions. Instead, it offers valuable insights into how you approach relationships, providing a foundation for growth and deeper self-understanding.

— — —

Beyond Childhood: Ongoing Life Events

While our early years lay the foundation for our emotional tendencies and attachment styles, it's also worth mentioning that our journey of development doesn't end with childhood. Life continues to shape us, and significant events in adulthood can profoundly influence how we perceive and engage in relationships.

Just as our childhood experiences created the initial blueprint for our understanding of love, trust, and connection, major life events in adulthood can reinforce these patterns or catalyze change. Consider the following scenarios:

1. **Professional Setbacks**: A failed business venture or unexpected job loss can shake our sense of self-worth and security. For someone with an avoidant attachment style, such an event might reinforce beliefs about self-reliance and the risks of depending on others. Conversely, it could be a wake-up call that leads to seeking more support.

2. **Romantic Relationships**: Our first significant romantic relationships often serve as a testing ground for the attachment patterns we developed in childhood. The end of a first love, for instance, can be particularly impactful. If the relationship ends painfully, it might confirm existing fears about intimacy and rejection. On the other hand, a healthy first relationship could begin to heal earlier attachment wounds.

3. **Loss and Grief**: The death of a loved one or the end of a long-term relationship can profoundly alter our emotional landscape. Such losses might trigger abandonment fears in those with anxious attachment styles or reinforce emotional distancing in those with avoidant dispositions. However, loss can also open us up to deeper connections as we seek support and comfort.

4. **Major Life Transitions**: Events like moving to a new city, changing careers, or becoming a parent can challenge our existing emotional frameworks. These transitions often require us to adapt our relational approaches and can be opportunities for growth in our attachment styles.

It's important to note that these adult experiences don't occur in isolation. They interact with our existing emotional patterns, often in complex ways. The ongoing nature of development also brings hope. It means that regardless of our childhood, we have continuing opportunities to grow and develop more secure ways of relating. Every significant life event offers a chance to re-examine our beliefs about relationships and potentially make positive changes.

— — —

Breaking Cycles and Creating New Patterns

To grow beyond old habits, you need to challenge your perceptions of threat and gradually open yourself to new experiences of connection. You must learn to bring subconscious influences into conscious awareness, allowing you to make different choices.

As we develop self-awareness, we gain insight into our own mind and the minds of others, allowing us to understand relationships with clarity and intention. The more emotionally aware we become, the less our emotions unconsciously drive our behaviors.

Remember, your beliefs about vulnerability and intimacy are not set in stone. The power to change rests with you. Your past doesn't limit you—your commitment to your future does, serving as the bridge between desire and action.

In the upcoming chapters, we'll delve further into strategies for recognizing and overcoming early programming. We'll explore ways to build more fulfilling connections in both your personal and professional life and challenge limiting beliefs.

Reflection Questions

1. What childhood experiences have most influenced your approach to relationships and emotional intimacy?

2. How would you describe your current attachment style? Can you identify specific behaviors that reflect this?

3. What beliefs or stories about relationships might be limiting your capacity for fulfilling connections?

4. How do you typically respond to moments of emotional stress or intimacy in your relationships? Are these responses serving you well?

PART II

— — —

Neuro-Emotional Intelligence:
Your New Competitive Edge

THE NEUROSCIENCE OF EMOTIONS AND DECISION-MAKING

Neuro-Emotional Intelligence 101

Have you ever wondered why you sometimes make decisions that don't seem logical, even to you? Or why certain situations trigger strong emotional reactions that feel beyond your control? The answers lie in the fascinating world of your brain.

Welcome to the realm of Neuro-Emotional Intelligence (NEI). This field merges neuroscience, psychology, and emotional intelligence to understand and manage the interplay between our brain functions and emotions. Our brains are wired for both emotion and reason, and these systems are constantly interacting to determine how we perceive the world and respond to it.

It's not just about having feelings—it's about how those feelings subtly guide your thoughts and decisions, often without your awareness. Your brain is constantly balancing emotions and logic to generate your experiences and behaviors.

This is why, to truly understand human behavior, we need to explore both psychology and neuroscience, and the relationship between them.

Even Ray Dalio, in his book *Principles*, emphasizes the importance of neuroscience, stating, "I attribute as much of my success to what I've learned about the brain as I do to my understanding of economics and investing."[17]

Here are some primary aspects of Neuro-Emotional Intelligence to keep in mind as we dive deeper:

- NEI helps us understand how different parts of our brain, like the amygdala and prefrontal cortex, work together to shape our emotional responses, behavior, and decision-making.
- By developing NEI, we can become more aware of our own emotional states and learn to regulate them effectively, leading to better decision-making and emotional balance.
- NEI isn't just about understanding ourselves—it also enhances our ability to empathize with others, improving our relationships and social interactions.
- NEI shows us how our emotions and thinking processes are deeply interconnected, helping us solve problems more effectively and boost our overall mental well-being.
- Ultimately, NEI bridges the gap between what we feel and what's happening in our brains, giving us powerful tools to navigate our emotional landscape with greater skill and understanding.

— — —

Key Brain Structures and Functions

As we consider the key structures that shape both emotional and cognitive processes, keep in mind that these are generalizations; the brain doesn't have specific circuits for every emotion or task. Multiple areas often work together for different experiences, and emotions manifest differently from person to person. As research advances, our understanding of the brain's complexity continues to evolve.

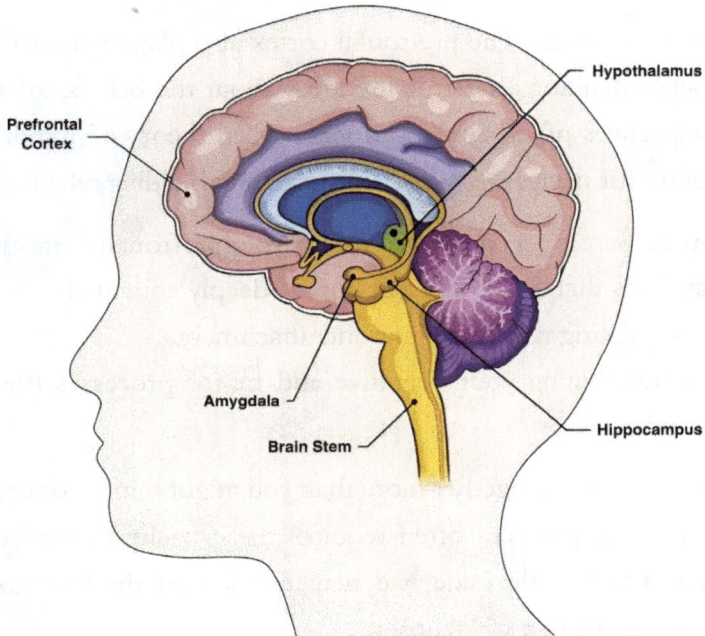

Figure 1. The Brain

THE PREFRONTAL CORTEX: YOUR BRAIN'S CEO

Imagine your brain has a CEO. That's your prefrontal cortex, located at the front of your brain. This is the part of your brain that makes you uniquely human, enabling you to imagine, create, and project into the future. It's in charge of:

- Setting goals and directing your actions
- Working with other parts of your brain to manage emotions
- Interpreting the past, understanding the present, and planning for the future

In line with its CEO duties, think of the prefrontal cortex as your brain's control center and integration hub. It pulls together information from various brain regions and your environment, helping you make sense of your experiences and your life as a whole.

But that's not all. The prefrontal cortex also plays a crucial role in your social cognition, constructing ideas about the beliefs, intentions, and perspectives of others in a process called theory of mind.[18] This is necessary for navigating social situations and building relationships.

Here's where it gets really interesting: your prefrontal cortex juggles two main jobs that seem different but are deeply entwined:
1. Regulating your emotions and attachments
2. Coordinating your cognitive and motor processes (thoughts and actions)

These two work together more than you might think. For example, solving a tricky problem often requires the capacity to regulate our emotions. On the flip side, we may use logical thinking to calm ourselves down when we're upset.

Your prefrontal cortex also gives you the amazing ability to reflect on your own thoughts and memories—that's called metacognition. This allows you to observe your stream of consciousness and analyze our own thinking processes, integrating emotions and cognition.[19]

One more fascinating fact: the frontal lobe, which includes the prefrontal cortex, doesn't fully develop until we're in our mid-twenties. This helps explain why teenagers often engage in risky behaviors—their brain's "control center" is still under construction!

THE LIMBIC SYSTEM: YOUR EMOTIONAL HEADQUARTERS

If the prefrontal cortex is your brain's CEO, the limbic system is its heart. This is where your emotions come from, and it plays a huge role in your decision-making. While your prefrontal cortex makes plans and gives instructions to the rest of the brain, your limbic system provides the inner strength you use to exhibit virtues like courage, forgiveness, and doing the right thing when it's hard. Let's explore its key parts:

THE HIPPOCAMPUS: YOUR MEMORY MAKER

The hippocampus, a seahorse-shaped structure found on both sides of the brain, helps you form new memories and identify potential threats. The hippocampus flags negative events, storing them front and center for future reference. This explains how you can forget the details of an event, but still remember exactly how you felt. The details of the memory may fade over time, but the emotions tied to it often stay just as strong as when you first felt them.

The hippocampus is constantly updating, keeping track of what's going on around you. However, this constant vigilance, combined with the amygdala's tendency to generalize threats, can sometimes make you feel more fearful or anxious than necessary. Your brain might see danger in situations that only vaguely remind you of past negative experiences.

THE AMYGDALA: YOUR EMOTIONAL ALARM SYSTEM

Picture two tiny, almond-shaped structures deep in the middle of each hemisphere of your brain. These are your amygdalae, and they're your emotional watchdogs. They're constantly assessing your safety, both physically and emotionally, comparing present situations to past experiences. This means that your emotional responses could be affected by both present circumstances and past events.

Your amygdalae develop before you're even born, which makes you capable of experiencing intense physiological states of fear even before birth.[20] These early, unconscious memories can later manifest as sensory, motor, and emotional recalls. The amygdala's connections to other brain regions amplify the impact of fear by triggering intense somatic arousal. This explains why some emotional reactions might seem disproportionate to the current situation—they may be triggered by subconscious memories. In addition, when your amygdala reacts very strongly to someone, it triggers a biological reaction that prevents your frontal lobes from fully receiving what they are saying and adjusting your thoughts or beliefs accordingly.

The amygdala is great at generalizing. For example, one bad experience with a spider might make you fear all spiders. This tendency to generalize can be both helpful and challenging. It helps you quickly identify potential threats, but it can also lead to distorted thinking and unnecessary fear responses. The hippocampus helps balance this by aiding in discrimination, recognizing that not all similar situations are equally dangerous. However, when your amygdala is triggered and you feel fear, you are unable to activate the learning and memory circuitry of your hippocampi. This means that fear can affect your perception, altering what you see (or think you see).

It turns out that the amygdala's influence extends beyond fear. It plays an important role in building social connections. As Daniel Coyle explains in his book, *The Culture Code*:

"When you receive a belonging cue, the amygdala switches roles and starts to use its immense unconscious neural horsepower to build and sustain your social bonds. It tracks members of your group, tunes in to their interactions, and sets the stage for meaningful engagement. In a heartbeat, it transforms from a growling guard dog into an energetic guide dog with a single-minded goal: to make sure you stay tightly connected with your people."[21]

However, it can also learn to associate positive stimuli, like praise or affection, with fear if past experiences were painful. This explains why some people may feel anxious in close relationships despite desiring connection.

Your amygdalae aren't directly connected to the parts of your brain that handle speech. That's why you often feel emotions in your body before you can put them into words.[22] However, the act of naming emotions can actually decrease amygdala activity and engage your prefrontal cortex.[23] This explains why talking through difficult situations or practicing mindfulness can be so beneficial in managing emotions.

HYPOTHALAMUS: YOUR BODY'S CONTROL CENTER

This tiny structure is like your body's control room. It sits just above the brainstem and signals the body to generate many of the visceral and hormonal changes that frequently accompany emotion.[24] It manages things like your body temperature, hunger, thirst, and sleep patterns. It's also involved in regulating sexual behavior and aggression.

Additional Neurochemicals to Consider:

1. **Oxytocin: The "Cuddle Hormone"**

   Oxytocin, often called the "bonding hormone," is produced in the hypothalamus and released by the pituitary gland. It plays a big role in:

   - Bonding with others
   - Influencing trust and social behavior
   - Childbirth, breastfeeding, and parent-child bonding
   - Romantic attachment and falling in love

Oxytocin interacts significantly with limbic structures, particularly the amygdala, affecting emotional processing and stress responses. It can promote feelings of trust and attachment by reducing the amygdala's answer to threatening stimuli.

Physical touch, like hugging, can trigger oxytocin release, potentially creating feelings of emotional closeness. Even positive social interactions without physical contact can boost your oxytocin levels.

2. **Dopamine: Your Brain's Reward System**

   This neurotransmitter is all about pleasure and reward. It:

   - Makes you feel good when you achieve something
   - Drives motivation and pleasure-seeking behavior
   - Measures how well rewards meet expectations

But here's the catch: if your brain gets too much dopamine too often (like from drugs or excessive thrill-seeking), it can start to need increasingly intense experiences to feel the same level of pleasure. As the brain adapts to frequent dopamine surges, less stimulating activities may lose their appeal, potentially decreasing overall life enjoyment.

To counter this, it's beneficial to engage in a variety of activities with different stimulation levels to maintain a balanced dopamine system.[25]

Understanding these brain structures and neurochemicals provides insight into the complex exchange between our emotions, thoughts, and behaviors, forming the foundation of Neuro-Emotional Intelligence.

— — —

How Your Brain Processes Information

DUAL PROCESSING THEORY: SYSTEM 1 & SYSTEM 2

Now that we've explored the brain's hardware, let's look at how it analyzes information.

Psychologist Daniel Kahneman distinguished between two modes of thinking: System 1 and System 2. These systems aren't isolated; they're constantly interacting in our daily lives.

As we discussed in Chapter 2, your brain is an anticipation machine; it's constantly making predictions about what's going to happen next, based on past experiences and current sensory input. This predictive processing is a core function that underlies both System 1 and System 2 thinking.

Let's look at how these systems typically work together.

SYSTEM 1: THE AUTOPILOT

This is your brain's automatic, rapid-response mechanism. It's characterized as:

- Automatic
- Rapid
- Effortless
- Instinctive
- Reactive
- Impulsive

Most of the time, your fast-thinking System 1 is running the show. It's quick, efficient, and requires less energy than System 2—perfect for routine tasks. For example, when you're driving a familiar route, System 1 handles most of the work. You don't consciously think about every turn or traffic light; it happens automatically.

System 1 also kicks in to make split-second decisions to keep you safe, prioritizing speed over accuracy—an essential survival mechanism. This explains how you can react to danger milliseconds before you're consciously aware of it, such as ducking to avoid a flying object before you even realize what's happening. The speed of System 1 is remarkable: the time between an emotional trigger and our reaction can be a fraction of a second.

However, this speed comes at a cost. System 1 relies on instinct and past experiences, which can lead to errors in judgment. It processes information quickly but lacks the nuance of rational analysis, especially when your self-awareness is compromised. This rapid response often overrides more thoughtful decision-making, which can cause problems in complex or unfamiliar situations.

System 2: The Manual Control

System 2 is your brain's slower, more analytical thinking mode. It's characterized as:

- Reflective
- Cognitive
- Systematic
- Rule-based
- Deliberate and conscious
- Focused on thinking and concentrating

You engage System 2 when you're solving a complex problem or planning a detailed project. While it's more accurate than System 1, it requires much more energy and effort, which is why it only activates when necessary.

System 2 can correct System 1's errors, but it doesn't always take charge right away. This can lead to misjudgments in situations where:

- System 1 reacts instinctively based on past experiences, even when they don't apply to the current situation.
- System 1 simplifies the problem by substituting a quick, related question when it can't find an immediate answer.
- System 2 tends to endorse System 1's suggestions without thorough examination, especially when we're tired, distracted, or overloaded.

This dynamic explains why you might have a strong emotional reaction to something before you've had time to think it through logically[26]—because System 1 takes the lead. System 2 steps in to provide more deliberate oversight only when the situation demands it, such as when an event doesn't align with System 1's expectations. For example, if you encounter an unexpected roadblock while driving your usual route, System 2 will activate to help you problem-solve and maneuver around it.

In essence, System 1 and System 2 are constantly working together to help you navigate the world, but understanding when to rely on each one can make a big difference in the quality of your decisions.

— — —

Emotions and Decision-Making: You're Less Rational Than You Think

In its effort to keep you safe, your brain constantly scans your environment to ensure your basic needs are met before shifting to other tasks like processing information, regulating emotions, and planning for the future.

Sometimes we pride ourselves on making decisions based purely on logic, but the truth is, emotions play a much larger role in our choices than we often realize or want to admit. In fact, it's frequently hard to tell where our feelings end and our "rational" thoughts begin.

Your emotions don't just exist in your mind—they affect your entire body. For instance, anxiety can raise your blood pressure, while happiness can boost your immune system. This intimate connection between brain and body means that even when you think you're being purely rational, your emotions are influencing you in ways you might not recognize.

As Ray Dalio notes, "The biggest threat to good decision making is harmful emotions."[27] When faced with a decision, your brain doesn't just engage in logical analysis. Instead, it draws on a wealth of information:

1. Physical sensations in your body
2. Emotions you're experiencing
3. Logical reasoning
4. Your subjective interpretation of reality
5. Unconscious drivers
6. Existing beliefs

The less aware you are of these factors, the more they influence you outside of your conscious control.

Why "Going with Your Gut" Isn't Always the Answer

Your gut feelings are sometimes your brain's lighting-fast reactions based on past experiences. When something happens, your brain doesn't just record the event—it registers signals from your entire body. Did your heart race? Did your muscles tense up? Your brain then associates these physical sensations with the memory of the event.

The next time you encounter a similar situation, your brain essentially runs an analysis against this emotional database and says, "I've experienced a similar sequence of physical sensations before." This can trigger emotions and reactions based on past experiences, even if the current situation is actually quite different. Though sometimes helpful, this can also lead you astray, especially if your past was traumatic or misleading.

When Emotions Take the Wheel

Think back to a time when you acted impulsively and later found yourself wondering, "What was I thinking?" This is a classic example of your emotional brain taking the wheel before your rational mind has a chance to catch up. Daniel Goleman explains this phenomenon in his book, *Emotional Intelligence*:

"Actions that spring from the emotional mind carry a particularly strong sense of certainty, a by-product of a streamlined, simplified way of looking at things that can be absolutely bewildering to the rational mind. When the dust settles, or even mid-response, we find ourselves thinking, 'What did I do that for?'—a sign that the rational mind is awakening to the moment, but not with the rapidity of the emotional mind."[28]

This effect is amplified when we feel threatened or stressed. Stress is a major culprit in activating emotional triggers. It reduces your brain's available bandwidth, limiting your capacity for awareness and intentional action. Under stress, you're less likely to employ newly learned coping tools or behaviors. Instead, your brain often defaults to old, automatic responses in a misguided attempt at efficiency.

In such states, your emotional brain can take control, distorting your perceptions and intensifying your reactions. You're more likely to:
- Focus on negative information
- Blow small problems out of proportion
- Struggle to see others' perspectives
- Find it harder to think creatively or see the big picture

This is why early experiences, especially in close relationships, have a profound impact on how you react to situations as an adult. If your early lessons taught you that getting close to others leads to pain, your brain might sound the alarm in intimate situations, even when there's no real danger. Your decision-making process is far more complex than you might realize, involving a delicate connection between emotions, past experiences, and rational thought.

The Cost of Compartmentalizing

As a high performer, your highly active, analytical mind often keeps you trapped in your head—analyzing, planning, problem-solving—leaving little time for self-reflection and feeling. Many of my clients resist exploring their emotions, especially emotions tied to past experiences, because they're afraid of opening up a can of worms they can't close. They think if they can effectively compartmentalize, they're in control.

But treating your inner world as something to put away and not look at actually sends a powerful message to your brain: whatever is in there must be so overwhelming that it's dangerous to examine. It's like hearing a suspicious noise outside your house at night but refusing to investigate—you end up building more anxiety around what must be so terrifying that you'd go to such lengths to avoid it.

Your body isn't designed to be in a sustained state of stress and suppression. It will inevitably manifest its discomfort somewhere: physical pain, sleep disruption, disordered eating, burnout, isolation, addiction, infidelity—the list goes on. In all my years, I have never met an addict whose addiction wasn't rooted in a deeper pain. You are designed to feel your emotions, and attempting to bypass them can derail your mental health at its most basic levels.

When you avoid processing difficult events, you might feel temporary relief, but you're actually hindering the neural integration necessary for healing and growth. This avoidance can keep you trapped in your past.

Consider Marcus, a highly successful entrepreneur whose story might sound familiar. Growing up, his family struggled to make ends meet. His parents were so focused on putting food on the table that they didn't have much energy left to offer warmth or reassurance. This left Marcus to rely solely on logic and reason, hindering his emotional development.

As an adult, Marcus approaches everything, including his marriage, with a strategic lens. This emotional detachment has led him to cheat on his wife periodically as a coping mechanism, though she either doesn't know or chooses not to acknowledge it. When we met through a mutual friend, Marcus was curious about the work I do but hesitant to engage deeply. He worried that exploring his emotions might mess up the careful system he'd built to keep his life under control.

I understand—when you've spent years building walls to protect yourself, taking them down can feel scary. I told Marcus what I tell all my clients: the path to understanding yourself better will always be there when you're ready to take it. It will be up to him to decide when avoiding the path is no longer an option.

Our brains are incredible, constantly juggling survival instincts, thought patterns, and emotional responses. When we understand how these pieces work together, we can make better choices and engage in relationships more skillfully. The question is: do you want to be in the driver's seat, or are you content as a passenger?

— — —

Characteristics of the Male Brain

While every brain is unique, there are distinct differences in how male and female brains process experiences. These are broad generalizations, and individual variations are significant. Not all men will exhibit these traits, and many women may display some of these characteristics as well. Still, recognizing these tendencies can help you better understand and manage your reactions, especially in emotional or high-stress situations. Some common inclinations in male brain processing include:

1. **Problem-Solving Focus**

   Many men tend to show care by trying to solve problems. When the male brain identifies an emotion, particularly in others, it often quickly shifts into action mode to address the issue. This can sometimes lead to misunderstandings in relationships, especially when a partner is seeking empathy rather than solutions. For high-performing males, this problem-solving approach can trigger rejection sensitivity if their attempts to "save" a partner or "fix" a situation aren't well-received.

2. **Anger Processing**

   Some men experience what scientists call "autocatalytic" or self-reinforcing anger. As Louann Brizendine describes in her book, *The Male Brain*:

   "Once some men's anger ignites, it's hard to stop. Their anger gets fueled by testosterone, vasopressin, and cortisol. These hormones reduce a man's physical fear of the opponent and activate his territorial fight reaction ... Scientists have found that when anger reaches the boiling point in some men, under conditions of high testosterone, it can produce pleasure, egging them on and making their anger harder to control."

3. **Competitive Drive**

   In men with higher testosterone levels, there's often a stronger need to dominate and a more dramatic reaction to being challenged. Higher testosterone levels can make the brain feel more invigorated and battle-ready in competitive situations.[29]

4. **Emotional Expression**

   Male brains also process emotions differently, sometimes leading to challenges in expressing feelings verbally. Brizendine notes:

   "The female brain tends to run negative scenarios to protect itself from disappointment and then place the blame on the male brain, like pinning the tail on the donkey. Constant criticism takes its toll on the brain. When a man's partner is critical of him, his brain goes on the defensive. His RCZ [rostral cingulate zone—a key brain region that is involved in free choices] tells him that he isn't meeting her mark, and he begins to avoid contact."[30]

In high-performing males, these reactions are often amplified. Due to your sensitive nature, the emotional aftermath can be draining, further distancing you from your partner and increasing feelings of pain and isolation. You then view this as validation for the tendency to shut down.

— — —

Neuroplasticity: The Brain's Capacity for Change

Your brain has an amazing ability to change and improve itself. This is known as neuroplasticity—your brain's natural capacity to rewire and adapt throughout your life. While your early experiences have influenced your mental "operating system," you aren't confined to those original settings. Your brain continually forms new connections, enabling you to develop new skills and ways of thinking at any stage in your life.

You can actively participate in this rewiring process, though it takes practice. It requires reflection and self-awareness, which may feel demanding at first. However, with conscious effort, you can alter your emotional responses and develop healthier ways of thinking and behaving. By connecting this to your values and deeper sense of meaning, you'll find greater motivation to persist.

As you become more aware of your reactions, you can make more intentional choices about how you respond to life's challenges. It's like being able to rewrite your own code—by shifting your perspective and consciously reframing emotional memories, you can even change how your brain stores them.

Having support throughout this journey—whether from a friend, mentor, or therapist—can make a huge difference. They can help you see situations from new angles, interpret old experiences differently, and establish healthier habits. Think of it as having a growth partner who can spot you when the mental lifting gets heavy.

Your brain's flexibility means that even though past experiences have significantly shaped your brain's structure and function, they don't have to define your future. With consistent practice and patience, you can create new mental pathways, change old habits, build better relationships, and make decisions that align with who you want to become. Each time you catch yourself in an old pattern and choose a different response, you're strengthening new neural connections. It might feel uncomfortable at first, and that's normal—that's your brain adapting.

Remember, this is about building strength over time. Give yourself permission to start small and progress gradually. Just like you wouldn't expect to squat 200 pounds on your first day at the gym, be realistic about the time it will take to build these new mental muscles. The payoff is worth it: better emotional control, stronger relationships, and the confidence that comes from actively shaping your own growth. Your brain's capacity for change opens endless possibilities for personal development, healing, and self-improvement. Now is the time to put that potential to work.

Reflection Questions

1. How can neuro-emotional intelligence allow you to better integrate your emotional and logical self?

2. Can you identify specific instances when your brain's "predictive nature" has led to incorrect assumptions in your personal or professional life?

3. How thoroughly are you taking into account all factors (such as your emotions and physical sensations) when making a decision?

4. How has understanding the characteristics of the male brain helped you make sense of your past reactions or behaviors in relationships?

CHAPTER FOUR

MASTERING EMOTIONAL INTELLIGENCE

In today's rapidly evolving world, where information is at our fingertips, cognitive abilities alone no longer guarantee success. Emotional intelligence, or EQ, has emerged as a critical factor in personal and professional growth—especially for high-performing individuals who often rely on intellect rather than emotion.

Emotional intelligence is the ability to recognize, understand, and manage your own emotions, as well as to perceive and influence the emotions of others. Unlike IQ, which measures cognitive abilities, EQ gauges your ability to navigate the complex social and emotional dynamics that affect every area of life. It encompasses self-awareness, self-regulation, empathy, and social skills.

— — —

Why EQ Matters in Today's World

As our society has evolved beyond basic survival needs, our potential for innovation has increased, but so has the demand for emotional intelligence to manage new challenges:

1. Workplace transformation: With the rise of remote work and increased job mobility, flexibility and strong interpersonal skills are essential.

2. Seeking meaning: People now look beyond financial compensation, seeking purpose and fulfillment in their work.

3. Navigating the AI era: With information easily accessible, success requires adaptability, critical thinking, and EQ to complement cognitive abilities.

— — —

The High Performer's EQ Challenges

High-performers, especially those with higher IQs, face unique challenges in developing EQ. The very traits that contribute to your professional success—rapid cognitive processing, a focus on efficiency, and strong problem-solving abilities—can hinder your ability to slow down, relate to others, or tune into the emotional nuances of social interactions.

These challenges often manifest as:

1. **Low Empathy**
   - Difficulty imagining or connecting with others' emotional states
   - Focusing on solutions rather than emotional understanding

2. **Difficulty with Social Connection**
   - Challenges in small talk or casual conversations (e.g., cutting off an employee's personal story to return to work tasks)

- Difficulty reading social cues and nonverbal communication

3. **Impatience with Others**
   - Impatience with those who process information more slowly
   - Frustration with delays or inefficiencies

4. **Resistance to Vulnerability**
   - Perceiving vulnerability as a weakness
   - Maintaining emotional distance as a defense mechanism

5. **Overreliance on Logic**
   - Difficulty balancing analytical thinking with emotional awareness
   - Undervaluing emotions in decision-making and interpersonal interactions

6. **Emotional Suppression**
   - Shutting down, lashing out, or turning away from emotions
   - Redirecting emotional expression in unhealthy ways

It's important to note that you often don't actually lack self-awareness or empathy; rather, you've developed patterns of self-preservation that create this perception. It's not that you're unaware of how others perceive you and your challenges in connecting with them. In fact, you're usually quite attuned to these dynamics. Instead, what others interpret as low empathy or indifference is typically a sophisticated defense mechanism to maintain emotional distance. You may choose not to engage emotionally, not because you can't, but because past experiences have taught you that avoiding vulnerability is safer or more efficient. Although this approach may seem to protect you, it can ultimately become a barrier to developing genuine connections and improving your EQ.

Despite these challenges, mastering EQ is crucial for high performers to level up in both personal and professional spheres. By approaching EQ development with the same strategic thinking and dedication applied to other areas of life, high performers can turn emotional intelligence into a powerful complement to their existing strengths.

— — —

The Power of Self-Awareness

Emotions always serve a purpose, and the only way to genuinely understand them is to grow your awareness of where they come from and what they're trying to communicate. Think of self-awareness as an internal compass that helps you navigate your inner world. Your body is constantly sending you messages through physical sensations: confidence might show up as better posture and steady breathing, while anxiety can appear as shallow breathing or a racing heart. Identifying these signs is a step toward self-awareness—the foundation of emotional intelligence.

But self-awareness goes beyond physical sensations. It helps you understand how your past experiences and personal biases affect your perceptions and reactions. As we've established, your early years mold your emotional responses and how you interpret events. If you grew up in a home where expressing emotions was discouraged, you might struggle to articulate your feelings as an adult. But recognizing this in yourself gives you the power to change it. As Carl Jung wisely said,

"Until you make the unconscious conscious, it will direct your life and you will call it fate."

The path to self-awareness starts with noticing your emotions as they arise and leaning into them rather than turning away from them. This openness helps you approach your feelings with curiosity instead of judgment. You begin to spot trends in your reactions, understand what triggers them, and connect them to past experiences. And you create the opportunity to learn healthier ways to manage your feelings and relate to others. The better you understand yourself, the better you can understand others.

Mindfulness is an important part of developing this honest understanding of what makes you tick. When your heart says one thing and your head says another, it's often just different stories playing out in your mind. By recognizing these competing narratives and what drives them, you gain the authority to consciously choose how you want to respond rather than acting on autopilot. This awareness—of your physical sensations, emotional patterns, and personal history—frees you from automatic reactions and helps you respond to life more intentionally. In Chapter 6, I'll share practical mindfulness tools to help you put this into action.

— — —

Emotional Intelligence and Influence

Emotional intelligence plays a major role in our ability to influence ourselves and others, as well as in how we're influenced by those around us. This dynamic can be visualized as three interconnected circles:

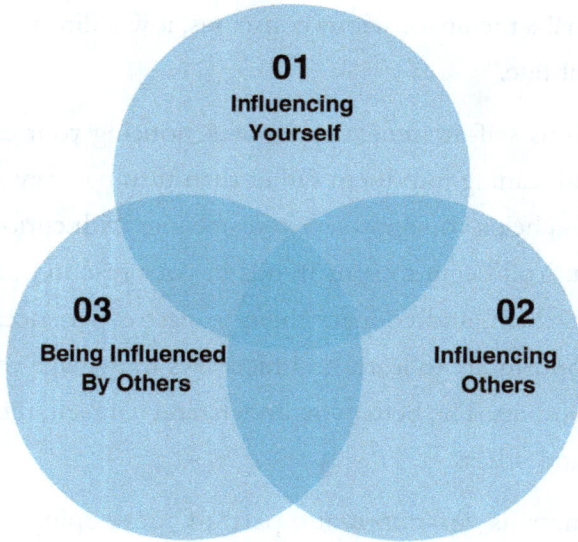

Figure 2. Influence and Emotional Intelligence

1. **Influencing Yourself:** Your ability to influence yourself is shaped by your fears, history, and interpretations of events. The key to creating influence and prompting action in this circle is self-awareness and control, extending to your thoughts, physical body, emotions, and expressions.

Effective strategies:

- Honor your emotions by listening to them without judgment, approaching them with curiosity and openness.
- Challenge automatic interpretations of physical sensations and emotions, considering alternative explanations for your feelings.
- Maintain a sense of agency, especially as a high-performer. High performers typically resist being changed, but are open to change they choose.

- When stepping into change, remind yourself that you've chosen this path, reinforcing your sense of control.
- Reassess your values from the perspective of your authentic self rather than your defensive self, using them to navigate difficult choices and resist old habits.

2. **Influencing Others:** Your capacity to influence others is rooted in your self-control, which is rooted in your ability to influence yourself. When you can manage your own emotions effectively, you're better positioned to positively influence those around you.

Remember:
- Your emotions set off a chain of events in how they affect other people, what those people do as a result, and how you respond in turn.
- Self-awareness is critical, giving you greater clarity on what you're doing, why you're doing it, how to regulate it, and how it's affecting others.

3. **Being Influenced by Others:** This circle represents how external factors—people and events—can trigger or heal you emotionally. This is where your triggers and your healers live, which are the people and events that either trigger or heal you. A person can fall into both categories as we build time and experience with them.

Emotional intelligence lives at the intersection of these three circles. Circle 1 requires you to be aware of yourself, Circle 2 requires you to regulate yourself, and Circle 3 expands to awareness of others and how their reactions, influenced by your behavior from Circles 1 and 2, impact you.

THE DEEPER CONNECTION BETWEEN INFLUENCING OTHERS AND BEING INFLUENCED

The relationship between how we influence others and how they influence us operates on multiple levels:

Physical Connection: Our brains are inherently social organs, designed to sync with those around us. In close relationships, this synchronization extends to our physical states—affecting heart rates, blood pressure, and emotional states. As neuroscientist Tali Sharot notes, "Emotion promotes brain synchronization."[31] While sharing thoughts takes effort, feelings transfer almost instantly. This is why your emotional state can dramatically impact those around you, and vice versa.

Mental and Behavioral Patterns: Our minds are constantly seeking coherent stories that explain our world. When we feel confident about something, it's usually because we've created a story that makes sense to us—whether or not that story is actually true. We tend to act in ways that confirm our existing beliefs, both about ourselves and others. For example, if you believe someone doesn't respect you, you might interpret their neutral actions as disrespectful, which then influences how you behave toward them, potentially creating a self-fulfilling prophecy.

Developing your emotional intelligence enhances your ability to navigate these spheres more effectively, creating a dynamic interplay between self-awareness, self-management, and social awareness.

— — —

Leading from the Heart

Emotional intelligence in personal relationships also extends to professional leadership. Leading from the heart isn't just about personal connection; it's about showing up authentically, cultivating trust, and setting standards in your work.

When you have the honor and privilege of touching people's lives and affecting their destiny, there is a sacred responsibility that comes with that. You give up the luxury to take the easy route and avoid what's difficult, and instead are charged with setting the highest examples of personal and professional behavior. A leader's essence is projected onto everything and everyone they lead. Most of your impact comes from who you are, rather than what you know or do. This is evident in the culture you cultivate. When leaders show up fully, fostering trust and making us feel valued, we become more willing to go the extra mile for them. Because our brains are wired to detect inauthenticity, this cannot be faked.

As Tim Spiker shares in *The Only Leaders Worth Following*, "Just as a tree is dependent on its roots for health and growth, so too is the effectiveness of what the leader does dependent on who the leader is as a person. Just as it is impossible for the tree to reach its potential without healthy roots, it is impossible for leaders to reach their full potential without being Inwardly Sound and Others Focused."[32]

Here's how you can apply these principles in your role as a leader:

1. **Nurturing your own needs:** Real leadership requires deep self-awareness of and comfort with who you are. When parts of you are longing to be seen or acknowledged, it hinders your ability to show up fully for others. By nurturing your own needs and embracing all aspects of yourself, even the challenging

ones, you'll be better equipped to inspire genuine growth in others and lead with authenticity.

2. **Connect to your heart:** Leading from your head is managing; leading from your heart is inspiring. The only way to inspire others is to be genuinely connected with your own heart.

3. **Walking your talk:** The more fully and sincerely you live, the more you inspire those you lead by modeling the way and showing what's possible. It is much harder to ask people to follow you where you aren't willing to go yourself.

4. **Being vulnerable:** Leadership is a relationship that often requires you to encourage and mobilize others. This level of action won't happen without making people *feel* something. To positively impact others, you must create an environment of safety and trust.

5. **Connecting to a cause larger than yourself:** Research shows that knowing our work is contributing something to the world yields higher performance and more motivation.[33] As Daniel Pink notes in his book, *Drive*, "The most deeply motivated people—not to mention those who are most productive and satisfied—hitch their desires to a cause larger than themselves."[34]

Leadership, both in relationships and business, is about influence, not control. It's about creating an environment where both you and others can thrive. Consider the ripple effect: How you show up affects those you lead, their teams and families, and, ultimately, a broader community.

***

Mastering emotional intelligence can profoundly alter every aspect of your life. For high-performing individuals, developing EQ unlocks new levels of success and fulfillment, helping you:

- Understand and manage your emotions more effectively
- Build deeper connections and stronger relationships
- Navigate the emotional complexities of modern life with resilience and grace
- Make decisions that align with your values and long-term goals
- Adapt to change and thrive in uncertainty
- Establish and maintain a greater sense of inner peace
- Allow yourself to be more vulnerable to strengthen trust and intimacy in relationships
- Lead with greater impact and inspire others

The goal is progress, not perfection. Each step you take towards greater emotional intelligence is a step towards a more balanced and content life—one that not only benefits you but also positively influences those around you, creating more emotionally intelligent environments in your workplace, home, and community.

In a world that increasingly values how we relate to others and navigate social and emotional complexities, developing emotional intelligence will set you apart. Embrace this path with curiosity, compassion, and courage, and you'll gain greater self-awareness, stronger relationships, more effective leadership, and deeper personal fulfillment.

Reflection Questions
1. When do you most often find yourself suppressing emotions, and what triggers this response?

2. How has your intellectual strength hindered your emotional connections with others?

3. In what situations do you tend to prioritize problem-solving over emotional support?

4. How does your leadership style change when you're under pressure versus when you're feeling balanced?

5. Think of a recent conflict—how might the outcome have been different if you had approached it with more emotional awareness?

PART III

— — —

Transforming Your Life (No-Nonsense Edition)

CHAPTER FIVE

THE COURAGE TO CHANGE

Your emotional experience is unique as a high performer. Your circle of connections is small, and those you truly trust enough to "let in" are few—sometimes nonexistent. Add to that the fact that with a packed schedule of high-level commitments, you're much busier than the average person, and that the world offers an abundance of distractions that make it easy to avoid the challenging work of introspection. This combination of factors leaves you with few opportunities to do the emotional work we're discussing. You might question whether this work is worthwhile, fearing that addressing old wounds could slow you down and keep you from achieving all that you desire.

But here's the truth: you're human. No matter how high-functioning you are, you're not exempt from basic human needs. In fact, because you're "different," you often have a greater need for genuine connection. This is emotional work, not logical work. Intellectual understanding alone isn't enough; you need to feel the deep emotional resonance of your behaviors to achieve lasting change.

— — —

The Nature of Change

Change is never easy, especially when it involves confronting long-held patterns and beliefs. These patterns have shaped you for years, and unlearning them can feel overwhelming. Yet, it's through this challenging process that you discover your truest self, opening up to deeper connections and a more gratifying life.

I always tell people, unless you're willing to do the difficult work of healing from your past, do not begin the work of self-awareness. So long as you are using your avoidant coping mechanisms, you've got that stuff tucked away. Your defenses are deeply ingrained because, as far as your brain is concerned, they've served you well—you're still here, right? But once you start opening the gates of empathy, vulnerability, compassion, courage, and self-love, there is no turning back. What's important is learning to recognize when these defenses are holding you back versus when they're truly necessary. Replacing them with healthier behaviors takes conscious effort and practice.

While your old habits may have offered some comfort, they were built on previous interpretations of your experience. As you shed them and embrace new ways of being, it's like a caterpillar emerging from its cocoon to become a butterfly. As the caterpillar sheds its skin, the head capsule—the part most tied to its identity—is the first to come off. In essence, it has to release a part of itself that it has clung to in order to gain its wings and become all it's meant to be. During this process, it can't even fathom the concept of wings or flight. As often attributed to Einstein: "I must be willing to give up what I am in order to become what I will be."

Change becomes necessary when the pain of staying the same outweighs the comfort of familiarity. For you, as a high performer, this change comes from accessing that next-level gear you have that most people do not. You might choose not to take on this work, and that's okay. Many people continue to hold onto what they know, even when it no longer serves them. But recognizing this as a choice empowers you to take responsibility for your life instead of feeling like a victim of circumstance.

While you consider the path ahead, think about the difference between happiness, which is fleeting, and joy, a lasting state of being. Often, when people wonder why they aren't happy, they look for things to change—their environment, their looks, their job—rather than behaviors to change. You may do things that make you feel happy in the moment, but it's your behaviors that create meaning and belonging that can lead to lasting joy and allow your heart to find a sense of "home".

In all my years of experience, education, and research, I've found that nothing inspires development more than love and empathy—both for yourself and others. This includes healthy self-love, love for a child or partner, spiritual devotion, and the empathy received from others that allows you to feel seen and human, not judged or criticized. When paired with self-compassion and driven by a genuine hunger for growth and transformation, these elements create the ideal conditions for meaningful change.

— — —

Taming the Ego

One of the biggest obstacles in your journey is likely going to be your ego. Every time your heart tries to communicate with you, your ego steps in, trying to protect you from the discomfort of vulnerability. It says, "What if I'm judged? Rejected? Seen as weak? Misunderstood?"

The ego blocks love and empathy, breeding more ego, whereas silencing your ego allows for the healing, trust, and connection necessary for growth. Defenses rooted in ego create a false sense of control, driven by fears and unconscious triggers. True control comes from greater awareness, giving you more options and freedom for how you behave.

This work is not about eliminating your ego but rather aligning it with your heart to serve your spirit's needs. The heart is far more powerful than the ego, which is why the ego has to work so hard to compete with it.

When you calm your ego, you're no longer in constant defense mode, allowing you to see beyond yourself. This shift is significant because dedicating yourself to something greater is key to finding meaning and purpose, leading to joy and fulfillment.

What often prevents you from opening yourself up to intimacy and vulnerability is your ego's need to be right, or the blind spots you have—though, in reality, they aren't as blind as you might think. The ego is frequently another mask fear wears in exchange for courage.

In *Humility is the New Smart*, authors Katherine Ludwig and Edward Hess identify four fundamental behaviors that help us overcome our limitations: quieting the ego, managing our thoughts and emotions, reflective listening, and emotionally connecting with others.[35] Setting aside our ego helps create the space for the rest of those things to happen.

One of my clients, Brian, the CEO of a beverage company, is a prime example of how ego can block connection. Highly intelligent, Brian had developed a habit of dismissing most people, including his leadership team, unless they proved themselves equally sharp. Even in our coaching sessions, his ego manifested as constant testing and questioning, needing to verify whether I was "worth his time."

Despite having done some self-awareness work and possessing decent emotional intelligence—he could recognize his feelings and those of others—Brian struggled to translate that awareness into emotional connection. He would often dominate conversations, and even when it was clear the other person had checked out, he couldn't stop himself from talking. Beneath this behavior were deeper triggers: his long monologues stemmed from insecurity and fear of rejection, affecting even his relationship with his wife.

However, Brian's story also shows us the possibility of change. Despite his initial ego-driven tendencies, he was fundamentally kind and generous, always ensuring that beyond his shortcomings people were treated fairly. As he worked through his imposter syndrome and developed strategies to calm his overactive mind, he became more secure. By slowing down, listening more, and doing the work to understand what drove his behavior, he was able to create space for new ways of being that allowed him to quiet his ego when necessary so his more endearing qualities could come through.

It's difficult when you realize that the ego, which has helped you navigate challenges in the past, can often stand in your way. When your brain sees people as another challenge to conquer, it does what has worked in the past: it activates the ego. But that very defense mechanism often undermines your ability to self-regulate, listen, and connect. When you free yourself from the struggle between self-preservation and self-acceptance, new opportunities emerge.

- - -

The Journey of Change: Stages and Challenges

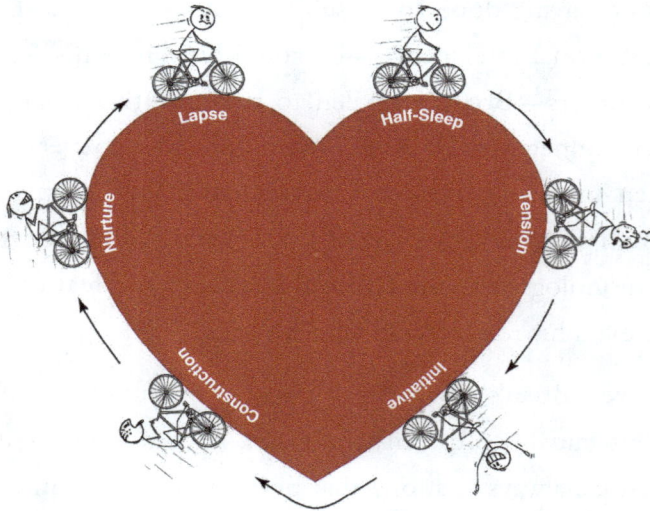

Figure 3. Essence Journey

Change is not a linear path but a cyclical journey. By understanding the stages of this journey, you can better navigate the challenges and setbacks that are bound to occur. Figure 3 above, explained below, is a model that illustrates some of the common phases of the cyclical process of change. It starts with what I refer to as the "Half-Sleep State" and moves clockwise:

Essence Journey

1. **Half-Sleep State**: You exist without reflecting on whether your current life is truly fulfilling.

   Example: Despite feeling a persistent nagging sense that something is off in your life, you dismiss these feelings and carry on with your usual routine. You might experience denial ("Everything is fine"), anxiety, and depression without clear root causes, resistance to examining your situation more closely, and a general sense of confusion.

2. **Tension Phase**: Growing discomfort creates urgency to examine your life more honestly.

   Example: You start feeling more frustrated and unhappy because the usual ways you cope with stress aren't working anymore. This can make you anxious, depressed, or angry. You might also feel skeptical and impatient, wondering if you can really trust the urge to make a change. Despite these feelings, the discomfort drives you to think more deeply about your life's purpose and what truly matters to you.

3. **Initiative Phase**: You start to build momentum as you uncover more about yourself and ask important questions.

   Example: You feel more energized and optimistic about the possibility of positive change, but you still struggle with uncertainty and self-doubt, wondering if you really have what it takes to make these big changes in your life.

4. **Construction Phase**: You start doing the hard work of growing, healing, and creating a new foundation for yourself. It can be stressful and frustrating, but you also begin to feel more open, accepting, and clear about your path.

Example: You commit to regularly reflecting on yourself, getting help from a coach or therapist, and developing new habits and ways of thinking. There are challenges, but slowly you start to feel more self-aware and emotionally balanced.

5. **Nurture Phase**: The changes you've made start to feel more natural and become a regular part of your life. You feel more at peace, hopeful, and clear about who you are and where you're going. You keep nurturing your growth by staying consistent with the self-work.

   Example: You've made self-care and personal growth a regular habit, helping you feel more grounded, purposeful, and in tune with your values. You're better able to handle life's challenges with grace.

6. **Lapse Phase**: Old habits can sometimes resurface, even after making progress. But these setbacks become shorter and less debilitating over time.

   Example: After a period of feeling stable, a big life stressor causes you to slip back into old habits or coping methods. But instead of staying stuck, you quickly get back on track and return to your healthier routines.

The point is to view change as an ongoing, cyclical process. There may be setbacks, but each cycle takes you deeper. The journey is about reconnecting with your "essence," so you can move through uncomfortable emotions and limiting beliefs to make space for growth.

— — —

Roadblocks to Look Out For

As you work to make positive changes in your life, you're going to encounter various obstacles and forms of resistance. Recognizing them can help you navigate them with more intention. Here are some common scenarios:

1. **Denial of Emotions**: You might find yourself saying, "No, I really don't feel empty," or "No, I'm really not sad that she left." This unwillingness to let yourself feel can be a significant roadblock. It's sort of like pouring water from a bottle while looking away: the longer you ignore it, the bigger the mess. Suppressed emotions build pressure in the psychological "system," creating emotional blocks that eventually find release through maladaptive behaviors or manifest as physical symptoms.

2. **Relapse and Losing Faith**: You start making genuine efforts to change, and those around you begin to notice and respond positively, lowering their defenses. But in a moment of weakness, you fall back into an old, destructive pattern. This slip doesn't just affect you; it impacts those who were starting to trust your change. They might think, "I knew it was too good to be true," and begin to pull away. Feeling hurt and discouraged by their reaction, you might then think, "Why did I even bother trying to change? It's pointless." This self-defeating thought leads you to abandon your efforts and revert to your old ways, thus sabotaging your own progress.

3. **Expecting Others to Change**: Just because you've decided to heal your past, open your heart, and embrace vulnerability

doesn't mean the people in your life will change their defenses or be open to your new ways immediately. You may also realize that expanding your consciousness and growing beyond your old ways doesn't automatically inspire those around you to do the same. It can feel discouraging when partners don't share the same level of awareness or interest in growth.

4. **Rushing Through Growth**: When revisiting painful experiences from your past, you might feel an urge to rush into action or "get to the point" rather than patiently allowing the process to unfold. You're likely used to a more results-oriented approach—"Hurry up and tell me how to do this, and I'll knock it out of the park!" However, this journey requires gentleness and patience.

5. **Fear of Being Overwhelmed**: My clients often tell me they suppress certain emotions and compartmentalize others because they believe that's what's required to do their jobs. They worry that feeling all of their feelings might derail their focus and energy.

6. **Resisting Calmness**: If you're used to chaos or negativity, prolonged calm can feel unsettling. Your brain might subconsciously create problems or seek out stress to return to its comfort zone.

7. **Falling into Complacency**: Once you start living in alignment with your deeper self, it's easy to become complacent. You might stick to minimal effort, like a few minutes of daily meditation, thinking you've done enough. You scratch the surface, feel "better," and think you're good to go. But just like

physical health, mental and emotional health require consistent effort and attention.

— — —

Hacks to Keep You On Track

As you become aware of the roadblocks that can interfere with your efforts, it's a good idea to equip yourself with strategies to navigate them successfully. Here are some practical ways to support your growth:

1. **Work with a One-on-One Accountability Partner**

   Seek support from a coach, therapist, pastor, or mentor who can offer a safe, trusting environment while challenging you to grow. This person acts as a guide, helping you navigate difficult territory, providing a judgment-free space to explore your thoughts and feelings while counteracting self-sabotaging tendencies. Many high performers resist this support, believing they can handle things on their own. But just like you'd hire a trainer at the gym, having someone guide your personal growth is equally valuable. That said, finding the right match is crucial. Unfortunately, anyone can call themselves a "coach," so do your homework and choose someone who takes the responsibility seriously. Your chosen guide needs to keep up with your quick thinking, understand the nuances of your personality, and handle your high ego and intensity. Don't waste time with an ill-fitting coach, but give the process a fair chance. Avoid relying solely on romantic partners for this role, as they may have their own biases and emotional involvement. An impartial third party focused on your development can be invaluable.

2. **Establish a Support Circle**

   In addition to an accountability partner, create a small group of trusted individuals who provide a non-judgmental, accepting environment. These people should hold you accountable to being your best self while offering diverse perspectives. A support circle offers collective wisdom and shared experiences, providing a broader network than a one-on-one partnership. It allows you to learn from others, creating a rich environment for progress. And it fosters a sense of community and belonging, which is critical for personal growth. To build this circle, be open about your desire for change and vulnerability. Invite others to challenge you constructively. Practice asking for what you need and encourage open feedback. And be prepared to adjust group dynamics as needed to maintain a positive, supportive space for all members.

3. **Design Your Environment for Success**

   Change your environment or routine to make positive changes easier and negative behaviors more difficult. For example, if you routinely stopped at the local bar on your way home to drown your emotions in alcohol, try taking a different route home. Or if you previously coped with stress by cheating on your partner when traveling, start a new habit of checking in with your partner each night when you're away. As Nick Saban says, "Every person has two things. You can do what you feel, or you can do what you choose."[36]

4. **Register Each Attempt**

   Take note of each effort you make towards your goals, and be mindful about how you frame them to yourself. For example, if you're trying to build trust in your relationship, acknowledge the steps you take to create more honest dialogue. You can even say out loud, "I'm doing this to build trust and strengthen our relationship." Notice how this language focuses on growth and positive action rather than self-criticism. Whether or not your partner notices and appreciates your attempts, recognize your own progress. This self-awareness helps your brain register that your new actions are meaningful, not just random behaviors, so you can move from introspection into intention and on to engagement. It also reinforces that you are in control of your choices, not being forced to make them. Each time you acknowledge these small wins, you create momentum that snowballs into growth.

5. **Separate Behavior from Self-Worth**

   Just because you've made mistakes in the past or engaged in behaviors you now regret doesn't mean you're fundamentally flawed. Your actions don't define your inherent worth as a person. If you find yourself identifying with past behaviors, use it as an opportunity to reframe. Instead of labeling yourself as "a failure" because you lost your temper, try saying to yourself: "I'm trying to become more patient and self-aware. I had a setback, and I know how to get on track again." This approach invites more self-compassion and provides the opportunity for you to focus on growth and improvement.

6. **Feel Your Feelings**

   The truth is that feeling your feelings doesn't have to knock you off course. Neuroscientist Jill Bolte Taylor's "90-second rule" suggests that the initial physiological response to an emotion only lasts about 90 seconds. Any lingering response beyond that is due to our choice to dwell on it.[37] This means that we have more control over our emotional states than we might think. By allowing ourselves to fully experience the initial wave of emotion without resistance, we can often move through it more quickly and effectively.

7. **Be Patient**

Think of the Moso bamboo: for months, even years, you water it without seeing it sprout. It looks like nothing is happening. Then, one day, it breaks through the surface, suddenly shooting up 20 feet in a matter of weeks. How is this possible? Because all that time, it's been quietly building a complex root system and storing energy underground. Your growth may feel the same—invisible at first, yet showing up subtly in your language, perspective shifts, and how you handle situations. Imagine yourself patiently sowing seeds that require time. Rather than rushing to fix your emotions, observe them. This patience builds resilience, making you more receptive to what arises, rather than numbing or suppressing feelings. Allow your emotions to be fully felt and understood. Just because you don't see immediate results doesn't mean progress isn't happening beneath the surface. One day, you'll look up and realize you're different. This process does not come in a pill or a prescription, and there are no shortcuts.

8. **Keep an Open Mind**

George Bernard Shaw said, "Progress is impossible without change; and those who cannot change their minds cannot change anything."[38] Allow for new experiences without preconceived expectations. Approach new learnings with curiosity ("What else might be true? What else is possible?") rather than trying to prove them wrong. This openness will enable you to overcome confirmation bias and discover new possibilities.

9. **Be Introspective**

   Sustainable, compelling personal growth stems from intro-spection. This involves looking within yourself, actively listen-ing to your thoughts and feelings, and engaging in constant self-dialogue and questioning. During this inquisition, when you're confused about the answers, try reconsidering the ques-tions you're asking.

10. **Be Willing to Let Go of What No Longer Serves You**

    Growth often requires shedding old habits, beliefs, or even relationships that no longer align with your current path. This can be difficult, but holding onto things out of familiarity can prevent you from moving forward. Be open to reevaluating the parts of your life that may need to change, recognizing that letting go creates space for new opportunities and healthier connections. Growth means being willing to release what's weighing you down so you can evolve into the best version of yourself.

11. **Tie Goals to Values**

    Connecting your change efforts to your core values can pro-vide stronger motivation and commitment. We'll talk more about this in Chapter 7, but it's important to mention it now as a critical strategy.

12. **Focus On Short-Term Attainable Progress vs. Long-Term Perfection**

    Instead of aiming for distant, perfect outcomes, focus on immediate, achievable results. For example, rather than trying to be "completely zen and never lose your temper again," focus on "maintaining calm today."

13. **Redefine Pain and Pleasure**

    We often do things to avoid pain or gain pleasure. Our brains are hardwired this way and learn from painful emotions. But what if we're wrong about what actually makes us feel good or bad? Our perceptions can be limited by misinterpretations of past experiences. What you attribute pain and pleasure to persuades the choices you make. Sometimes, we avoid things that seem painful but could actually help us grow. For example, someone might avoid going to the gym because it feels hard, even though it's good for them in the long run. Or they might eat junk food because it tastes good now, even if it makes them feel bad later. To make real changes in your life, perhaps it's necessary to redefine what you see as "good" or "bad." This means looking at why you think certain things are painful or pleasurable. Try to see difficult but helpful actions as good things. View harmful habits as bad, even if they feel good in the moment.

14. **Start Now, Don't Wait for Perfection**

    The best time to start is now. Overcomplicating things can turn you off from beginning at all. Take a small step, do something, but start somewhere. Don't wait for certainty. You don't need all the answers to begin; you just need the commitment to keep going.

15. **Don't Let Setbacks Set You Back**

I cannot tell you how often I hear clients who are making an effort to do something different share stories of being shot down for what they didn't get right, leaving them wondering what the point of trying really is. This is especially true for those who tend to see challenges as proof that "this isn't working," leading them to revert to old defenses. But setbacks are normal and should be expected. Change is frequently a process of two steps forward and one step back, with inevitable bumps along the way. Do your best to view each setback as a learning opportunity. By reducing self-judgment, limiting beliefs, and negative self-talk, you minimize lost ground. When you mess up, be vulnerable. Be courageous. Be willing to say "I'm sorry," take ownership, and get back on track. Consistency over time leads to progress because you're trying to build new data sets in your brain and a primary way your brain does this is through repetition, just like when you're training a muscle or learning a new skill. This repetition eventually makes the behavior automatic, and because your brain seeks efficiency, it prefers this automaticity. The life that you live is fueled by the habits you develop, and resilience in facing these challenges is what ultimately leads to lasting change.

— — —

The Case for Change

True transformation involves challenging long-held beliefs and stepping into vulnerability. This may be the very thing holding you back from becoming who you're meant to be. It requires living according to your truest values, so you don't regret missing out on the best parts of life— because regret shows no mercy.

As you move toward personal reform, consider what you stand to gain—and what you risk by staying the same. Your emotions are influencing your actions whether you realize it or not, so why not take control? When your thoughts, behaviors, and feelings are anchored in the past, change requires unlearning old habits and developing new ones. You are not defined by your past unless you choose to dwell there. So, as you consider whether to take the next step, ask yourself: are you at peace?

Embracing change gives you the power to make choices that align with your authentic self, rather than being driven by subconscious emotions rooted in old stories. This shift reveals a profound truth: immediate "wants" often stem from fear or the desire for instant gratification, whereas true "needs" arise from self-awareness and serve your higher purpose.

As you deepen your connection with yourself and integrate the various facets of your being, you'll notice a stronger alignment between your core needs and surface desires. This leads to proactive (instead of reactive) living—designing a life that reflects who you truly are, rather than reacting to circumstances.

During this process, hidden truths will surface, fueling your motivation to continue. Each step forward and each insight gained builds momentum. Real change happens when you stop reacting to your emotions and start treating them as a rough draft—giving yourself the space to examine new perspectives and possibilities.

As a high performer, you're accustomed to excelling at most things, and this strength can make it difficult to confront areas where you lack expertise. But the most significant growth happens just beyond your comfort zone. Just as your professional success has come from taking risks, your personal growth requires taking risks, too. Lean into discomfort and unfamiliar territory; that's where growth happens.

Whenever you are confronted with something painful, you're at an intersection: you can either explore the truth it's revealing or settle for the temporary comfort of the illusion you prefer. Ironically, choosing the challenging route will lead you to a greater state, but we often hesitate to engage that discipline.

Reflection Questions

1. What defensive pattern do you most need to change, and what's one step you could take today?
2. When was the last time your ego prevented you from connecting with someone important to you?
3. Who in your life do you trust most to give you honest feedback about your blind spots?
4. Which of your current habits directly contradicts the person you want to become?
5. What truth about yourself are you avoiding through busyness or distraction?
6. If nothing changes in your life over the next five years, what would you regret most?

CHAPTER SIX

THE MIND-BODY CONNECTION— SOMATIC TOOLS

In a culture that often glorifies constant mental activity and endless to-do lists, listening to your body might seem foreign. Yet, the mind and body are deeply intertwined. If you are unable to recognize the translation between your physical and emotional feelings because you are detached from your emotions, you don't gain control, you lose it. Your body holds wisdom that can guide your emotional health, decision-making, and, ultimately, your ability to lead an authentic and fulfilling life. Tapping into this wisdom requires a shift in focus—from purely mental analysis to embodied awareness.

As we've already discussed, neuroplasticity is your brain's remarkable ability to rewire and adapt. Your brain can form new connections with intentional practice, allowing you to change old habits and build new ones. Neuroplasticity is the tool, but the real power lies in your willingness to engage with it daily. Through this work, you're not just changing behaviors—you're reshaping how you experience yourself and the world around you.

Now, let's see how to actively apply this in your daily life to support personal transformation. This involves becoming deeply aware of your emotions, bodily sensations, and automatic reactions. That awareness creates the gateway for healing and rebuilding.

In this chapter, we'll explore somatic practices that bring you back into your body, harnessing its inherent wisdom to foster personal growth. Whether you're aiming for emotional resilience, making better choices, or a deeper connection to yourself, these tools will help you get there. You don't need to master all of them at once—pick the ones that resonate most with you and incorporate them into your routine at your own pace.

One suggestion I offer clients is to create a literal "toolbox." This can be something simple, like an empty tissue box. Write the name of each tool on a piece of paper, place them in the box, and keep it visible as a reminder. When you are in need of a tool or preparing to practice, pull a paper from the box.

These tools are not meant to be rigid prescriptions but rather flexible guidelines that you can adapt to your unique circumstances. As you experiment and become more attuned to your body's signals, you'll likely discover variations that work especially well for you.

— — —

Tool 1: The Mindful Pause

One of the key steps in rewiring your brain is learning to pause. In this moment of pause, you slow down your automatic reactions, creating space to make intentional choices instead of reverting to ingrained behaviors. The pause allows you to step back and recognize patterns in your thoughts and responses.

For example, if your brain has internalized the belief that vulnerability isn't safe, it might instinctively trigger defenses whenever emotional openness is required. By pausing, you can notice this tendency rather than react automatically. Instead of a thought like, "Anyone I trust will betray me," you create the opportunity to reframe it with something more inspiring, such as, "Not everyone I trust will certainly betray me."

With practice, this tool helps you create space between stimulus and response, allowing for conscious actions rather than reactive ones. Slowly, each pause helps you break old patterns and strengthens your capacity for change.

How to practice:
1. When you feel triggered, just pause.
2. Notice any sensations in your body and what they might be telling you about your current state.
3. Take three slow, calming breaths.
4. Ask yourself: What words or actions would best serve this moment right now?
5. Choose your response with intention.

Practice time: Use this method throughout the day, especially in moments that test your patience or composure.

— — —

Tool 2: The Body Scan

Building on the mindful pause, the next step is to deepen your awareness by performing a body scan. This practice helps you tune in to the subtle cues your body is sending, which can offer valuable insight into what needs attention. By increasing body awareness, you can identify and interpret physical sensations that often go unnoticed, yet carry important messages about your mental and emotional state.

Whereas the mindful pause helps you break out of automatic reactions, the body scan provides clarity on what your body is experiencing and communicating. For instance, you may detect areas of tension, tightness, or even warmth and relaxation. These sensations can reveal emotions, such as frustration or calm, and allow you to respond to your unmet needs.

How to practice:
1. Find a quiet space and close your eyes.
2. Take three deep breaths to center yourself.
3. Start at your head and slowly scan downward through your body.
4. Notice any sensations, such as tightness, warmth, pressure, or ease.
5. When you find an area of discomfort, explore it with curiosity:
   a. What does this sensation feel like?
   b. Does it have a color or shape?
   c. What emotion might it connect to?
   d. What could this feeling be trying to tell you?

Practice time: This practice can be used at any time, and you can start with just 5 minutes a day.

As you become more attuned to your body, you'll start noticing trends—certain sensations might arise in response to specific emotions or situations. For example, after a heated argument with your partner, your mind may focus on thoughts like, "I can't believe they did that!" This triggers a physiological response, and a body scan might reveal tightness in your chest. Your beliefs about relationships then chime in, reminding you that getting close to others isn't safe because they can hurt you. This intensifies the physical reaction, reinforcing the cycle. By practicing the body scan, you deepen your awareness of these signals, helping you become more self-aware and better able to manage your responses.

To further enhance this tool, you might consider working with an experienced practitioner, such as a mindfulness coach or somatic therapist. These professionals can guide you through more advanced techniques and help you deepen your connection to your body's wisdom. They can help you develop a mental "safe space"—a calming refuge where you can retreat if the sensations become overwhelming. This safe space might be a peaceful beach, a serene forest, or any environment where you feel completely at ease, allowing you to feel grounded and secure as you delve into your emotions and physical sensations more fully.

— — —

Tool 3: Emotion Mapping

With Emotion Mapping, you take a deeper look at what your emotions and body signals are trying to communicate. Ignoring or suppressing your emotions is like ignoring a crying child—it only increases their intensity and makes them harder to manage over time. By learning to observe your emotions without judgment, you start understanding the messages they carry and how they relate to your body's responses.

This tool enables you to trace your emotions back to their sources and to create a more complete picture of your emotional landscape.

How to practice:
1. When you notice a strong emotion, pause.
2. Name the emotion without judgment.
3. See if you can locate where you feel it in your body.
4. Ask yourself: What is this emotion trying to tell me? What deeper need might it be uncovering?
5. Respond with curiosity.

Practice time: Use this tool whenever strong emotions arise, especially in moments when you feel triggered or reactive.

When you follow your emotions to their core, you'll start seeing patterns in your emotional responses. Anger, for instance, may signal that a boundary has been crossed or point to a deeper unmet need. By acknowledging and addressing the root causes, you reform emotions from sources of discomfort into guides for self-compassion and growth, helping you build a more grounded and resilient sense of self.

— — —

Tool 4: Feelings vs. Facts Check-In

This tool helps you distinguish between emotion-based thoughts and proven facts. Often, what feels like a fact is actually just a feeling with no real evidence to support it. A fact is something that can be proven true, like "My name is Leila." I have a birth certificate to show it. But statements like "I can't trust anyone" or "I'm not good enough" are feeling-based. We often hold onto these so firmly that our brain begins to treat them as truths and responds accordingly.

For example, saying "I'm afraid I might be hurt if I let my guard down" leaves space for possibility. But telling yourself "I *will* get hurt," creates a barrier. By checking whether a thought is a fact or a feeling, you open up possibilities that emotions alone may have closed off. Yes, you may have been hurt before, but do you know for certain it will happen this time? Can you prove it?

How to practice:
1. Take out a piece of paper and draw a line down the middle.
2. Label one column "Feelings" and the other "Facts."
3. Write down your thoughts, placing them in the appropriate column.
4. Remember: Facts must be provable (like "My name is Mark").
5. Feelings can't be proven (like "Letting someone get close to me is not safe").
6. Review how this list continues to change.

Practice time: 10 minutes daily.

This exercise helps you see where you might be holding onto beliefs that aren't grounded in truth. Keep in mind, however, while a feeling may not be a fact, it's still important to honor your emotions. They hold meaning and typically point to underlying needs. The goal isn't to dismiss your feelings, but to gain clarity so you can better address your actual needs.

— — —

Tool 5: Daily Meditation

Expanding on your emotional awareness and body mindfulness, daily meditation strengthens your ability to remain present and aware in your life. This practice improves your capacity to observe your thoughts and feelings without getting caught up in them, allowing you to respond intentionally rather than reactively.

Meditation offers profound benefits, including reduced stress and enhanced emotional regulation. Regular practice cultivates superior mental clarity and focus, sharpening your problem-solving abilities and broadening your perspective on challenges. Over time, meditation contributes to rewiring your brain and reducing the activation of the amygdala, which is linked to the fight-or-flight response. Research shows that meditation can increase gray matter in brain regions responsible for attention, empathy, and compassion, while decreasing activity in the brain's default mode network, associated with mind-wandering and rumination.[39] Rather than trying to shut down your thoughts, meditation helps you disentangle from them. It creates a solid foundation for self-exploration, allowing you to release resistance to past events or future worries.

To start your meditation practice, choose a quiet place where you won't be disturbed. Sit comfortably and focus on your breath, allowing yourself to let go of any judgments or distractions.

Simple Meditation Guide:
1. Find a comfortable seated position.
2. Set a timer.
3. Focus on your breath.
4. When your mind wanders, gently return your attention to your breath.
5. Be patient: It's called practice for a reason.

Practice Time: Start with any amount of time you are willing to try, gradually increasing as you feel comfortable.

Even though I've been meditating for decades, I still struggle with it at times. The key is to practice consistently. Even just five minutes a day can lead to significant changes in your brain, fostering a greater sense of calm and empowering you to navigate life's challenges with greater ease.

— — —

Tool 6: Awe Practice

Awe is more than just an emotional response; it offers significant benefits for both mental and physical health. Research indicates that experiencing awe can lower stress levels, enhance feelings of connectedness, and even reduce inflammation in the body. When you encounter awe, your body reacts in tangible ways—muscles relax, breathing becomes deeper, and a profound sense of peace envelops you. These physiological reactions create a powerful mind-body feedback loop, helping you transition from a state of stress to a state of presence and wonder.

To quote Albert Einstein again, "There are only two ways to live your life: as though nothing is a miracle, or as though everything is a miracle." Cultivating awe is about choosing the latter mindset—learning to see the extraordinary in the ordinary.

Daily Awe Exercises:
1. Spend time observing something in nature. Notice the intricate patterns on a leaf or watch the sky at sunrise or sunset.
2. Seek out new experiences, whether it's visiting a new place, learning something new, or meeting new people.
3. Engage with art, music, or literature that moves you.
4. Pay attention to acts of kindness or bravery in others.
5. Savor everyday moments, whether it's a cup of coffee, the sound of a wind chime, or a meaningful conversation.

Practice time: This is a great practice to engage in at any time.

The more you foster awe, the more you can shift your perspective and enhance your appreciation of the world around you.

***

Your body's wisdom and your conscious awareness form a powerful partnership in personal growth. At the heart of this partnership lies mindfulness—the practice of bringing your full attention to the present moment without judgment. As one of my teachers said,

"It's re-mindfulness, reminding us to be mindful." This mindfulness creates a foundation for all somatic practices.

As you incorporate these somatic tools into your daily life, you'll discover that they work synergistically: each practice amplifies the others. The mindful pause creates space for deeper body scanning, which in turn strengthens emotional awareness. This heightened awareness makes meditation more profound, and regular meditation practice makes it easier to distinguish between feelings and facts. Then, from this increased presence, a natural sense of awe emerges.

The beauty of mindfulness is that it can be practiced anywhere. Whether you're savoring a meal, hiking, gardening, or washing dishes, each moment becomes an opportunity to deepen your connection with yourself. This integration of mind and body goes beyond managing stress or processing emotions; it's about reclaiming your innate capacity for wholeness. By learning to listen to your body's signals and honor its wisdom, you develop a nuanced understanding of yourself and your needs, leading to more authentic choices and relationships.

Just remember, to make these tools effective, you have to practice them regularly. Like building any new habit, you need to start small, be consistent, and be patient with yourself. Some days, you might feel deeply connected to your body's wisdom; other days, you may struggle to maintain that connection. This ebb and flow is normal and part of the process. What matters is your commitment to returning to these practices, even after moments of disconnection. If you cannot learn to be at peace in the Now, your dis-ease will join you everywhere you go.

Reflection Questions

1. What prevents you from pausing before reacting in challenging situations?
2. How can deepening your somatic awareness serve you in your growth?
3. When you attempt meditation, what tends to be your biggest obstacle?
4. When was the last time you experienced awe, and how did it feel in your body and mind?

CHAPTER SEVEN

BECOMING THE ARCHITECT OF YOUR LIFE

The journey of personal growth and reformation is fundamentally about becoming the architect of your own life. It's about recognizing that while you can't change the events of your past, you have the power to reinterpret them and choose how they inform your present and future. This chapter will guide you through rewriting your story, returning to self-love, and embracing authenticity to create a life that aligns with your deepest values and aspirations.

— — —

Rewriting Your Story

In the blueprint of personal transformation, our narratives are the foundational plans we can choose to redesign. As the architect of your life, you have the power to reconstruct the stories that have defined your past, creating a more empowering structure for your present and future.

As we discussed in Chapter 2, the stories we tell ourselves about our experiences shape our identity and our reality. Often, these narratives allow us to feel seen, even if the only one acknowledging our experiences is ourselves. You crafted your version of events in the best way you knew how for self-preservation, and as the author of your story, you have the power to rewrite it. For instance, if you've long believed "I can't trust others to show up for me," that can lead to struggling with vulnerability and never asking for help. Reframing this to the likely truth that "There are people I can rely on to support me" opens up the door to deeper connection and mutual support, reducing feelings of isolation. When we reexamine and rewrite the beliefs and interpretations we've constructed, we unlock the potential for profound personal development.

To demonstrate this, let me share a story about the power of rewriting one's narrative. William, the CEO of a successful textile company, came to me reluctantly, urged by his board of directors. Though a charming and skilled negotiator, he struggled with his temper, interpersonal demeanor, and difficulty connecting with employees.

Through our work together, William opened up about his upbringing. In doing so, he came to understand the source of his struggles: a childhood marked by a hypercritical mother and an emotionally absent father. These early experiences left him feeling perpetually unseen and inadequate. The belief that emotions were unsafe and that getting too close to others would lead to disappointment followed him into adulthood, particularly affecting his relationship with his girlfriend, Brooke. Although he yearned for emotional intimacy, his defensive and self-protective behaviors created barriers to genuine connection.

Eventually, William began to recognize how his past had directed his current behavior. More importantly, he started to see that he had the potential to author a new narrative. The walls he'd built weren't actually keeping him safe; they were preventing him from experiencing the deep connection he desired. This insight led to meaningful changes in his relationship with Brooke. Instead of maintaining emotional distance, he learned to express his feelings and trust in the safety of vulnerability. Slowly, their relationship reformed from one characterized by emotional unavailability to one built on mutual trust and growing intimacy.

William's story reiterates a fundamental truth: it's not the events in our lives that sculpt us, but the beliefs we create about what those events mean. By reexamining these beliefs and the interpretations we've constructed, we put ourselves back in the driver's seat of our lives. As you expand your capacity to lean into your emotions rather than avoid them, you can begin to reshape your narratives with a mindset of acceptance rather than judgment.

If you'd like to try this now, reflect on a moment in your past that you've always interpreted negatively or tried to avoid recalling—perhaps it's a failure, a rejection, or a loss. Consider what other interpretations of the story may have been possible that would allow you a different perspective. Think about what opportunities you have to rewrite the story, how the experience served you, and how you can give yourself what it is you needed but failed to receive then, such as a sense of safety.

— — —

Connecting with Your Inner Child

Often, this process of rewriting your story begins with connecting to and healing your inner child. Remember that your childhood experiences were interpreted by a child's brain, not your current adult mind, which might be able to rationalize the past. It's the child's perspective of these stories that's significant and may need healing. By nurturing and validating your inner child, you begin to release the lingering feelings of powerlessness, fear, shame, or unworthiness that may have taken root. This healing process allows you to reclaim your inherent sense of worth, making you more genuinely confident and empowered. When you feel whole, you're no longer seeking external validation to prove your value—your confidence comes from within.

Imagine how you would talk to a child who is hurting. How would you comfort them? How would you show up for them? The best condition for a child's development is to be present with them, tuning in to their experience and being receptive to what comes up.

The child-state in you is no different. Because you may not have been properly attuned to as a child, you can tune in to your child self now through your own active presence of your internal experience as you notice what thoughts and feelings come up. You can identify what the child in you was needing to hear and feel, and deliver those messages to the child now.

If the term "inner child" feels too abstract or doesn't resonate with you, feel free to use alternatives like "emotional self" or "inner self." The concept remains the same, regardless of the terminology you choose. It's remarkable how difficult it is for most of my clients to show up for themselves in this way, even if they have their own children to help them imagine their child self.

— — —

Child's Truth Exercise

Try this exercise:

1. Close your eyes and imagine yourself as a child.
2. Recall a significant childhood story—perhaps a time when you felt scared, lonely, or misunderstood, including any sensory details you can recall.
3. While connecting with your younger self 's emotions, imagine giving yourself what it was you were needing at the time (for example, a supportive presence or a loving embrace). Through this imagination, you begin to rewrite the script for that experience.

You can also engage with your inner child by looking at childhood photos, talking to your younger self, or even playing. These can be helpful ways to jog your memory, especially for those of you who have trouble connecting with your inner child because you've blocked out or disconnected from the pain of the past.

For instance, imagine a family event where you fell and hurt yourself. Instead of comforting you, your parents scolded you for embarrassing them. Identify the childhood needs that weren't met— perhaps you didn't feel seen, safe, or cared for. What did you need but not receive in that moment? Maybe what you needed was for a loving parent to kneel down beside you and ask, "Oh honey, are you okay?"

Now, picture yourself as the adult in that situation. How would you comfort that child? Offer that comfort to yourself in the present moment. Can you feel both the pain of the child and the compassion of the adult? How does the child's pain change with this compassion? Instead of stuffing down the pain and masking it, can the child feel their emotions and simultaneously feel seen, safe, and held?

This exercise helps you inventory emotional experiences in your brain database, giving voice to feelings you've pushed down and blocked out, which initiates healing. Recalling these stories isn't about dwelling on the past or getting stuck there. The goal is to revisit the memory, offer healing, and file the memory away again—but with a healthier "tag" or perspective attached to it. As Wayne Dyer said, "I believe if you change the way you look at things, the things you look at change."[40]

When you revisit a painful memory, feel the associated emotions, and create a new narrative, you replace the pain with a positive experience and affect the impact of the trauma. You take charge as the author of your life, shifting power from your early experiences defining your fate to the realization that true power lies in taking responsibility for your story.

By reconnecting with these memories while staying grounded in your present self, you create a rhythm of leaning in, releasing, and healing. Over time, this transforms you from a victim of your past into the master of your future.

As you relax your grip on suppressing emotions, they loosen their grip on you. The space you create allows you to sit with a feeling as it arises, and in doing so, you're able to witness that feeling come and go, ebb and flow, rise and fall, and see that allowing yourself to experience emotions doesn't mean you're "stuck" in them.

As you engage in this process, it's not uncommon to begin having more dreams. Keeping a journal of these dreams and exploring dream interpretation (if you're working with a therapist or someone with appropriate expertise) can often reveal powerful insights.

Another significant effect of this work is the ability to shift your attachment style to a more secure one based on these new truths. As Amir Levine shares, "Research into the molecular mechanism of memory and learning reveals that whenever we recall a scene—or retrieve a certain memory to our conscious mind—we disrupt it, and by doing so, we alter it forever. Our current experiences shape our view of our past ones. By creating your own attachment inventory, you reexamine your recollections of past relationships from a fresh new perspective. Viewing them through an attachment lens will allow you to change some unhelpful beliefs that rely on those particular memories, and by doing so reshape your working model into a more secure one."[41] Resolving the past changes the present.

— — —

Witnessing and Integrating Emotions

An essential part of rewriting your story is learning to witness and integrate your emotions, rather than suppressing or avoiding them. This involves:

1. **Listening to your body**: Your body often holds wisdom that your conscious mind hasn't yet processed. Pay attention to your emotions and physical sensations and what they might be

telling you. Does your stomach tighten when you think about certain events? Do you feel a lightness in your chest when you consider new possibilities?

2. **Accepting all emotions**: Courage involves not only refusing to silence your emotions, but going further to examine them with acceptance and curiosity to understand how they inform the person you have become today. Emotions are neither good nor bad—they are valuable sources of information.

3. **Exploring the roots**: Take time to understand the stories that feed the person you are today. Learn how they have impacted you and the way you see the world. This might involve journaling, therapy, or deep conversations with trusted friends.

4. **Rewiring your brain**: Retell past and present stories from a new lens. This isn't about dissecting the stories of your past, but rather understanding how they inform your present. When you catch yourself falling into old patterns of thought, pause and ask yourself if there's another way to interpret the situation.

— — —

SET UP: A Tool for Emotionally Intelligent Decision-Making

To tie together some of the main ideas we've explored so far, I'd like to introduce you to the SET UP tool—an easy-to-recall acronym designed to enhance your emotional awareness and integration. This practical tool helps you take a quick inventory of your internal landscape. It can be particularly helpful when interpreting events or making decisions, offering clarity on what might be shaping your perspective. To move from reactive to intentional decision-making, check your SET UP. Approach your inquiry with curiosity and be open to what comes up.

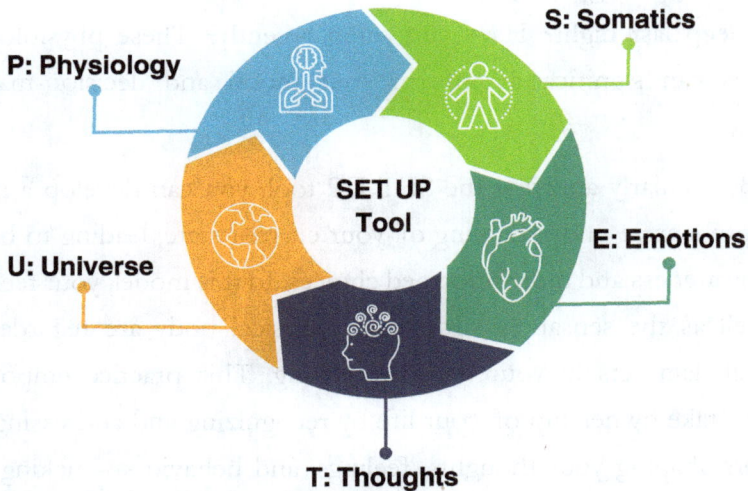

Figure 4. SET UP Tool

S: Somatics - Check in with your body for any physical sensations. Is your breathing shallow or rapid? Do you feel tense? Pay attention to what these bodily sensations might be alerting you to.

E: Emotions - Ask yourself what feelings are coming up for you in this moment. Are you feeling joy, anxiety, anger, or perhaps a mix of emotions?

T: Thoughts - What thoughts are running through your mind? Are they supportive or critical? Observe your thoughts without judgment.

U: Universe - Take an inventory of what else is in your universe at this time. Are you excited about an upcoming vacation? Are you frustrated about a recent disagreement with a loved one? Consider how these external factors might be affecting your current state, particularly if there's something you're avoiding.

P: Physiology - Consider your physiological state. How well did you sleep last night? Have you eaten recently? These physiological factors can significantly inform your mood and decision-making abilities.

By regularly applying the SET UP tool, you can develop a more comprehensive understanding of your current state, leading to better self-awareness and more informed choices. In this model, your feelings as well as the sensations from your physical body are regarded as critical data sets in your decision-making. This practice empowers you to take ownership of your life by recognizing and addressing the factors shaping your thoughts, feelings, and behaviors—making you the architect of your own journey.

— — —

Journaling for Growth

Journaling is a powerful tool for organizing your thoughts and emotions. Writing activates the narrator function in your mind, helping you give structure and language to chaos, stress, or emotionally charged events. This can reduce physiological reactivity to challenging experiences and create a sense of control that lowers stress. Here are some prompts and techniques to try:

1. **Reflective Letter**: Write about an experience from another person's perspective. For example, if you are in a disagreement with your significant other, try writing from their point of view, expressing their side of the story, and exploring how they felt.

2. **Protection Letter**: Write a letter to yourself, affirming that you are safe, protected, and more than enough.

3. **Forgiveness Letter**: Write a letter of forgiveness to yourself or someone else. You can write from your adult perspective or from the viewpoint of your younger self.

4. **Love Letter**: Express love openly and explicitly (beyond just "I love you") to yourself or someone else, again from either your child or adult perspective.

5. **Free Association Writing**: Set a timer for 60 seconds and write non-stop about a chosen word or topic. Afterward, review what you wrote and pick the word that evokes the strongest emotion, whether positive or negative. Then, free-write based on that word. You can repeat this process, choosing a new word each time. This method allows you to peel back layers of thought and uncover deeper associations that may be triggering your surface emotions.

Journaling doesn't have to be perfect. When clients struggle with journaling, it's generally because they're overcomplicating it by worrying about following a set method or having perfect grammar. Forget all that! The goal is to express and explore your thoughts and feelings, not to create a literary masterpiece.

— — —

Using the Past to Understand the Present

To live a more conscious, empowered life, you must explore the foundation of your past, understanding how previous experiences have shaped your current structure. This archaeological work reveals the underlying patterns that have unconsciously guided your life.

Understanding your past helps you view your present through a new lens. Ongoing challenges—like being triggered by colleagues, seeking constant approval, feeling inadequate, or struggling with relationships—often trace back to earlier experiences in your life. Most of your reactions emerge from your subconscious, making them difficult to recognize in the moment. This is why good decision-making goes beyond analyzing facts—it requires deep self-knowledge and emotional intelligence.

Self-analysis alone can be unreliable because you may have buried difficult truths behind protective beliefs. Your self-awareness may still be developing, and your childhood interpretations of events likely differ significantly from your adult understanding.

Keep in mind that your amygdala—the brain's emotional center—holds onto these early reactions. Rewiring these ingrained responses takes time and patience. Learning to step back and examine your feelings from new perspectives can help you overcome their hold on you.

— — —

Self-Compassion and Healing

Healing is not about demolishing your past, but about carefully reinforcing the structures that have been weakened by early experiences. Exploring your past can be uncomfortable, often stirring up feelings of shame, sadness, or anger. As you navigate this process, approach yourself with compassion, not judgment. This journey isn't about rejecting who you are, but embracing who you are now. Healing starts with accepting all of yourself and recognizing that your core essence is love, even if your past actions haven't always reflected it. True growth and transformation come from a place of compassion, not self-degradation. Self-criticism only creates more obstacles.

In uncovering the reasons behind your struggles with intimacy and connection, you might feel shame about past behaviors in relationships. You might feel sad when you recall the many times you've pushed others away, criticized them, or shut down. Grief may arise as you mourn lost opportunities.

Shame, in particular, is difficult to confront because pride often prevents us from admitting we feel it. Yet, shame diminishes our capacity for guilt, empathy, and self-reflection, which are essential for growth. As Dr. Louis Cozolino explains, "Shame needs to be differentiated from the later-occurring phenomenon of guilt. Guilt is a more complex, language-based, and less visceral reaction that exists in a broader psychosocial context. Guilt is related to unacceptable behaviors, whereas shame is an emotion about the self that is internalized before the ability to distinguish between one's behavior and one's self is possible. If guilt is 'I did something bad,' then shame is 'I am bad.'"[42]

Understanding this distinction offers hope. By allowing yourself to fully feel the grief of losing the emotional safety you needed as a child or by processing difficult adult experiences rather than avoiding them, you can gradually loosen pain's grip on you. Grief needs a witness for healing—an acknowledgment that your emotions deserve space and compassion. Grief needs you to surrender to your feelings, without rushing to fix or suppress them. This is what allows you to rewire your brain's architecture, influencing how you feel, react, and perceive the world.

Self-compassion serves you far more than self-esteem in the process of healing. It gives you the grace to accept your imperfections and approach your healing journey with patience. This compassionate self-awareness not only fosters emotional resilience, but also strengthens your ability to connect with others.

Ultimately, this work of self-compassion is what empowers you to face your pain and take ownership of your growth. Rather than seeing your struggles as something to overcome alone, you begin to understand them as part of the human experience. The relationships awaiting you after this inner work can offer deeper vulnerability, trust, safety, and love.

— — —

Positivity Practices

Becoming the architect of your life is about intentional daily actions that shape your mindset and foster emotional well-being. Try the following practices to help you design a life rooted in purpose and positivity.

GRATITUDE PRACTICE

Cultivating an intentional gratitude practice is a simple yet highly effective tool for shifting your perception and increasing overall well-being. Gratitude boosts dopamine and serotonin levels in your brain, and the point is not just to feel gratitude, but to express it.

How to Practice Gratitude:

1. Keep a gratitude journal, writing down three things you're grateful for each day, big or small.
2. Write gratitude letters to others, expressing your appreciation.
3. Listen to a gratitude meditation, focusing on things you're thankful for.
4. Share your gratitude verbally with others.

Don't overcomplicate this practice. I keep a gratitude journal that takes me no more than three minutes each morning. Even small things, like appreciating a comfortable pillow or a hot cup of tea, can become sources of gratitude.

FUTURE-SELF VISUALIZATION

This exercise helps you connect with your aspirations and motivate yourself towards positive change.

How to use it:

1. Find a quiet place where you won't be disturbed.
2. Close your eyes and take a few deep breaths to relax.
3. Imagine yourself 5, 10, or 20 years in the future, living your ideal life.

4. Visualize as many details as possible. What does your future-self look like? How do you carry yourself? What have you accomplished?

5. Now imagine your future-self giving you advice. What would you tell yourself about the journey ahead?

6. Open your eyes and journal about your experience.

This exercise can help you clarify your goals and give you motivation to work towards them.

— — —

Living Authentically

Authenticity aligns your inner blueprint with your external framework. By ensuring your actions reflect your core values, you create a life that is both structurally sound and personally meaningful.

Authenticity is rooted in an ongoing attunement to the self, void of the lies we tell others (and worse, ourselves). It means being free from the masks we often wear. When you live as your genuine self rather than an armored version, you become a better person, leader, friend, and partner. As Ernest Hemingway is often credited with saying, "There is nothing noble in being superior to your fellow man; true nobility is in being superior to your former self." The real challenge isn't outperforming others—it's overcoming what holds you back from fully expressing your truest potential.

This requires courage. It means being willing to be vulnerable, and showing up as yourself even when it's uncomfortable or scary. It means letting go of who you think you should be to embrace who you really are.

Kevin Cashman offers an important insight in *Leadership From the Inside Out*: "We are always authentic to our present level of development, but we may be inauthentic to who we could become."[43] This explains why few people recognize authenticity as something they need to work on; we're all behaving in alignment with our current level of emotional, psychological, and spiritual development. As a result, we may conclude that we are "authentic," doing the best we can with the knowledge, experiences, and competencies we have at this time. The catch, however, is that authenticity is not a fixed destination but a continuous journey of growth and self-discovery.

IDENTIFYING YOUR VALUES

One of the first steps toward living more authentically is understanding your core values. Your values are your internal compass, guiding your decisions and actions throughout your life. When you live in alignment with them, you experience more fulfillment.

You may notice that certain values have remained constant for years. For example, my top five are faith, love, gratitude, passion, and impact. I can look back and see how these values have been the driving force behind many of my actions and decisions over the past few decades.

It's important to note that your values differ from your beliefs. As Adam Grant says, "Who you are should be a question of what you value, not what you believe."[44] Your beliefs may evolve over time. For example, I may hold a belief that investing in the stock market is not for me, then change that belief over time. But your core values are much more foundational. A shift in values would require a significant catalyst.

When reflecting on your values, also consider who or what your "greater than self" might be. Is it your team? Those you mentor? Your family? This reflection is vital and must come from within. Your "greater than self" connects to your deeper sense of purpose and offers an essential layer to understanding your core values.

Take time to identify and rank your values in order of priority. They are the "why" that anchors your life with meaning. When the work gets tough and you question why you should keep going, your values will give you the strength to make the right choices instead of the easy ones.

VALUES VAULT EXERCISE

Identify your core values and use them as guiding principles for your decisions and actions. These values serve as an anchor for your life and help align your choices with who you want to be.

How to use it:

1. Take some time to reflect on what's truly important to you. Is it honesty? Creativity? Compassion? Adventure? If you feel unclear on your values, consider the choices you make when you're at your best and explore what drives them. For example, if you frequently adjust your work schedule to attend your daughter's soccer games, it might indicate family as one of your values.
2. Narrow it down to your top 5-7 core values.
3. For each one, write a brief description of what it means to you.

4. Regularly review your values and ask yourself if your actions are in alignment with them. I recommend printing them out and keeping them somewhere visible. Try reciting them out loud if it helps. I repeat mine daily as part of my morning routine.

IDENTIFYING AND CHALLENGING LIMITING BELIEFS

As you work to reengineer your inner landscape, you'll inevitably encounter internal obstacles that can impede your progress. These obstacles often take the form of deeply ingrained limiting beliefs—mental constructs that act like invisible barriers, preventing you from fully realizing your potential. Just as an architect must identify and remove structural weaknesses before building a strong foundation, you must recognize and challenge these limiting beliefs to create a life aligned with your true self. These unconscious narratives, often developed in childhood or through societal conditioning, can thwart your efforts at personal transformation if left unchallenged.

Common limiting beliefs include:
- "I'm not good enough."
- "I don't deserve success."
- "I can't change."
- "The world is a dangerous place."

By identifying and carefully deconstructing these barriers, you create space for new, more supportive structures of thought and belief. Once you're aware of a limiting belief, you can challenge it. Ask yourself:
- Is this belief really true?
- Where did this belief come from?

- How is this belief serving me?
- What would be possible if I let go of this belief?

***

Becoming the architect of your life requires courage, commitment, and compassion for yourself and others. It involves peeling back the layers of conditioning, societal expectations, and self-imposed limitations to uncover your true essence. This journey isn't always easy, but it's infinitely rewarding.

As you progress, you'll notice profound changes not just in yourself, but also in your relationships and your impact on the world around you. You might experience greater intentionality in your decision-making, enhanced resilience in the face of challenges, and a deeper sense of contentment. Your relationships will improve through better communication and deeper connections. Professionally, you may find yourself demonstrating stronger leadership skills and having a greater influence on those around you. Moreover, your personal growth journey can inspire others and lead to more meaningful contributions to your community.

Remember, you are more than enough. You have within you everything you need to become the architect of your life. Trust in your journey, be patient with your progress, and celebrate every step along the way. Your best self is waiting to emerge—all you need to do is give it the space and nurturing it needs to grow.

Reflection Questions

1. What story do you want to write for yourself?
2. How can you use the SET UP tool to optimize your decision-making?
3. How can you practice more self-compassion in your journey of personal growth?
4. What impact do you want to have on others and the world around you?
5. What decision can you make today that aligns with something greater than yourself?

PART IV

— — —

Leaning Into Love and Partnership

CHAPTER EIGHT

UNDERSTANDING RELATIONSHIP DYNAMICS

"The relationship between two people can be no healthier than the emotional health of the least healthy person."
—Dr. Neil Clark Warren

As a high performer, you've achieved great professional success, but you may find that the same skills don't always translate seamlessly into your personal life. Why does closing a big deal feel easier than opening up to a partner? How is it that leading a large team seems more straightforward than connecting deeply with one individual?

This chapter is your playbook for boosting your relationship game. We'll tackle why high performers often fumble in their personal lives and how to turn that around. You'll learn about the LAB Triangle, the power of vulnerability, and why self-reliance, while beneficial in many aspects of life, can become a barrier in relationships.

Get ready to apply your A-game to building connections that actually matter. It's time to score big in your personal life.

— — —

The LAB Triangle: Love, Agency, and Boundary

For high performers, having the right tools in a relationship can be highly influential. Just as you wouldn't attempt to build a skyscraper without a solid foundation and the proper equipment, you shouldn't approach your relationships without a framework for success. Enter the LAB Triangle—a powerful tool for understanding and navigating the intricate dynamics of healthy connections.

This model breaks down the core elements of any healthy engagement into three main components: Love, Agency, and Boundary. Understanding and balancing these elements can be the difference between a relationship that thrives and one that merely survives—or worse, crumbles under pressure.

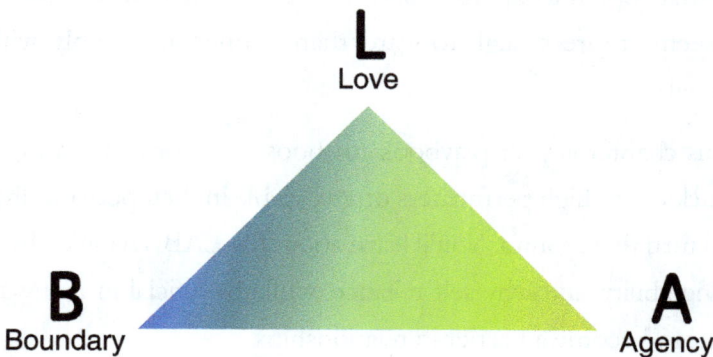

Figure 5. The LAB Triangle: Love, Agency, and Boundary

Let's break it down:

1. **Love**: This isn't just about the level of care someone feels for you and vice versa. It's about how openly you both express it, how deeply you each receive it, and whether it comes in a way that resonates with each of you.

2. **Agency**: This refers to the degree of freedom you each feel in making choices as opposed to feeling pressured into decisions. As a high achiever, you're accustomed to being in charge and calling the shots, so having a sense of control and agency in your relationships is particularly important. In addition, being in control is one of the ways in which you maintain a feeling of safety. People don't fear change itself—they fear being forced to change. The more you feel able to influence outcomes in your relationships, the more motivated and engaged you'll be.

3. **Boundary**: This represents your effectiveness in holding your boundaries and respecting those of your partner.

Any healthy relationship requires a balance of these three elements, including the relationship you have with yourself. When this balance is off, the relationship suffers.

Let's look at an example to illustrate this concept: Neil, a successful entrepreneur and national leader, was smart, resilient, and driven to excel. However, beneath his confident exterior, he was incredibly sensitive, battling shame, insecurity, and a fear of rejection. His defense mechanisms—shutting down, lashing out, and cheating—were keeping him from living the life he truly wanted.

Neil came to me curious about how he could improve as a leader. As we built trust, the conversation shifted to his personal life, where his challenges ran deeper. Though loved by his parents, Neil had longed for more emotional connection and safety from them. Early heartbreaks only reinforced his belief that love was risky, leading him to keep his intimate relationships at arm's length.

However, during our time together, Neil met a woman named Sara who he truly cared for. She set clear boundaries and encouraged him to choose his actions without trying to change him. Although Neil struggled to break old patterns, this relationship prompted him to confront his fears and begin to open up to the possibility of loving fully. It marked a turning point for Neil, helping him embrace his desire for connection and family. Although his journey was slow, Neil began inching toward living from his deeper self rather than his defensive one, opening up to the idea of loving someone wholeheartedly.

Applying the LAB Triangle:

1. **Love**: Sara expressed her love for Neil, and he continued to lean into expressing his love for her.

2. **Agency**: Sara never tried to force Neil to change or give him an ultimatum. She gave him the space to make his own choices, and maintained her authority to make hers.

3. **Boundary**: Sara held her boundaries with Neil rather than letting him overpower her, and since this was something Neil wasn't used to but he wanted to be with her, he was forced to search for new ways to be in the relationship.

As we continue to explore relationships, keep this LAB Triangle in mind. It will serve as a valuable tool for assessing and improving your relationships.

— — —

Intimacy Challenges for High Performers

WHEN SELF-RELIANCE BECOMES MALADAPTIVE

As a high performer, you're accustomed to projecting strength and competence. You know how to get things done, solve problems, and push through challenges. But this same drive for self-reliance that serves you so well in your career can become a major barrier to intimacy.

Psychiatrist Amir Levine explains: "Studies show that belief in self-reliance is very closely linked with a low degree of comfort with intimacy and closeness. In romantic relationships, it reduces your ability to be close, to share intimate information, and to be in tune with your partner."[45]

At the root of this challenge often lies a deeper fear of emotional pain, specifically, the pain of rejection. What makes rejection feel so devastating? Research shows that our brains process social rejection in the same regions that handle physical pain. That's why emotional hurt can feel as real as a physical wound. To shield yourself from this pain, you might unconsciously keep others at arm's length. While this might offer temporary relief, it only reinforces the fear, making genuine connection seem even more risky.

Many high performers mistake self-reliance for true independence. While it's important to stand on your own feet, when taken too far, this mindset cuts you off from vital emotional support and connection. It narrows your focus to just your own needs, leaving your partner's needs unmet. More importantly, it robs you of one of the most fulfilling human experiences: being part of something bigger than your-self through selfless love and deep, authentic connection—where both partners can give and receive openly, without the constant need for self-protection.

This overemphasis on self-reliance actually goes against our fundamental nature. Humans are inherently social creatures, wired for connection from birth. Our brains need human engagement to thrive and for healthy aging. In fact, the quality of our relationships is the single biggest factor in our long-term health and happiness, according to the Harvard Study of Adult Development, a 75-year longitudinal study.[46]

Imagine if you feared drinking water despite knowing its necessity for survival. You might limit yourself to the bare minimum, feeling constantly thirsty. Similarly, denying yourself the fullness of love dehydrates your soul.

Why You Push People Away (Often Without Realizing It)

If you recall, in Chapter 2, I gave an example of how avoidant attachment patterns can manifest in romantic relationships—those with avoidant tendencies often withdraw when intimacy increases. This push-pull dynamic isn't limited to romance. Despite the innate human need for connection, you may find yourself pushing people away in various types of relationships as a means of self-preservation. You might create a belief that allowing closeness is a greater threat than the unmet need for connection, and your protective instincts take priority.

Yet, the human need for connection still pulls you toward others. This creates a continuous cycle of running toward the very thing you're running from. If closeness truly didn't matter to you, you wouldn't experience this internal conflict—you'd simply push people away without hesitation. But because that need for connection exists, the emotional push-pull cycle continues.

These "push away" behaviors are physiological and psychological responses to fear, rooted not in being a bad person or disliking people, but in survival. When these behaviors arise from survival mechanisms, changing them can feel particularly challenging. Your mind argues, "Hey, I kept us alive, didn't I? So, it must be working." While that may have been true in the past, these same behaviors may not serve you in all future contexts.

A wise mystic once said, "The one who avoids having their heart broken will have their heart broken forever." In other words, avoiding vulnerability guarantees the very pain you're trying to escape.

Until you actively work to break this cycle of keeping others at a distance, it will persist. This deeply ingrained tendency often operates below your conscious awareness, making you feel the need to retreat even when you don't fully understand why.

THE HIGH PERFORMER'S RELATIONSHIP LOOP

As a high performer, you may find yourself caught in a repetitive cycle when it comes to intimate relationships. This loop frequently involves predictable behaviors and emotional reactions that can sabotage your connections. Let's look at five common obstacles—you may recognize some or all of these in your own experiences.

1. **Feeling Cornered by Emotional Demands**: When your partner urges you to share your feelings—especially during heated arguments—you may feel manipulated, coerced, or as if her focus is on easing her own pain rather than understanding yours. This perception can leave you feeling violated, drained, and frustrated, with the real issues still unresolved. The pressure to engage emotionally on someone else's terms can feel like a competition you're not equipped to win, making the false allure of a quick fix—like simply walking away—far more tempting.

2. **Lashing Out to Protect Yourself**: Your relationships may turn into emotional "boxing rings" where you lash out in an attempt to fight off your own inner demons. In these moments, you might project a defensive, "asshole" persona through anger, withdrawal, or harsh criticism. Your partner then reacts to this persona with her own means of coping, and the more vulnerable parts of you retreat even further, creating a cycle that reinforces your belief that love isn't safe. You begin to see suppressing your pain and expressing it as anger as the only way to protect yourself.

3. **Struggling to Nurture and Be Nurtured**: A friend once said, "We spend our whole life fighting for the nipple." In other words, we're all seeking something to nurture us. Everyone wants to love and be loved—it's a universal need. But in your case, you might feel emotionally blocked, as if you're trying to grow a garden of love by sprinkling seeds on hard, infertile

ground. Without rich emotional soil, the seeds of connection struggle to take root.

4. **Setting Unrealistic Expectations**: When you do allow someone to get close, the relationship can feel precarious because you let so few people in. You may hold this person to unrealistically high standards, expecting her to have extraordinary patience and resilience to break through your defenses and connect with the parts of you that long to be understood.

5. **The Cycle of Failed Relationships**: Eventually, these relationships tend to end. Either you walk away because you feel your needs aren't being met, or your partner grows tired of the pain and toxicity—tired of being tested and expected to love you unconditionally—and leaves. In response, you feel abandoned or rejected, reinforcing your belief that it's safer to stay in control than to be truly vulnerable and in love.

Self-Protective Behaviors that Sabotage Relationships

In addition to these obstacles, high performers often retreat from their partners in unconscious ways that further strain their relationships. These self-protective behaviors might seem helpful at first, but over time, they sabotage intimacy and connection. This retreat commonly stems from a need to escape distress, which you may experience as fear, pain, anger, or anxiety. Misidentifying the source of your discomfort leads to ineffective solutions that don't provide relief. Your emotional state can cloud your perception and decision-making, and though you're free to choose your actions, you can't always control the consequences. These self-protective behaviors may include:

Choosing Anxious Partners: You might repeatedly choose anxious partners, and their behavior reinforces your belief that deep intimacy isn't possible or safe. This dynamic allows you to keep your distance, protecting yourself from the risks of true emotional engagement.

Creating Unnecessary Conflict: You may pick fights over trivial matters or stubbornly argue, even when you know you're wrong. This behavior distracts from deeper, more vulnerable issues that feel too risky to address directly.

Shutting Down: Stonewalling, disappearing, or ignoring your partner are forms of emotional withdrawal that shield you from perceived threats but also prevent genuine connection.

Infidelity: Sometimes it's not that the better answer is too hard but simply that the wrong choice is too easy, and this is part of what fuels infidelity. Cheating can feel like a way to avoid full commitment, even at the cost of damaging a potentially great relationship. As Tony Robbins says, "Sometimes we treat the symptoms of a problem while we nurture the cause."[47] In addition, the brain has a powerful capacity to simulate experiences, allowing you to vividly imagine the relief or excitement infidelity could bring, but the temporary thrill rarely leads to long-term satisfaction.

Dishonesty: Dishonesty can take many forms, from lies and omissions to half-truths. Often, these are ways to avoid conflict or the fear of disappointing your partner. Your intelligence, quick thinking, hypersensitivity, and fear of vulnerability may lead you to lie almost instinctively. You might convince yourself that these lies are meant to protect others, but in reality, they protect no one—not even your sense of self. Dishonesty, especially when it crosses into secrecy, erodes trust and limits genuine intimacy. While privacy—such as keeping certain personal thoughts, feelings, or experiences to yourself in a healthy way—can nurture trust and strengthen emotional bonds, secrecy does the opposite. Secrecy involves withholding information with the intent to deceive or manipulate, creating a foundation for the gradual destruction of trust.

Making Excuses to Break-Up: You might find yourself looking for reasons to end relationships just as they become serious. The increasing intimacy may trigger your fear of vulnerability, prompting you to leave before you risk being hurt.

As we continue to explore the intricacies of emotional intelligence and relationship dynamics, recognize these behaviors as unconscious defense mechanisms that play a role in your decision-making. By identifying these relationship-sabotaging tendencies, you can develop better strategies for managing emotions and building more fulfilling relationships.

— — —

Shared Responsibility: It's Not All on You

Even as a high performer committed to personal growth, you may find yourself struggling to navigate the complexities of modern relationships. The truth is, these challenges aren't solely due to personal shortcomings—you don't have to carry the entire burden alone. Several societal factors also play a role in making it harder to form and maintain deep, significant connections. To name a few:

The Impact of Modern Hookup Culture

The rise of dating apps and the "swipe right" culture has normalized quick, surface-level connections. Although these platforms make it easy to meet new people, they often encourage instant gratification over the more meaningful relationships many of us crave. This can lead to shallow interactions that fall short of meeting our need for real intimacy and bonding.

A Lack of Positive Role Models

One significant challenge is the scarcity of exemplary relationship models in our society. You might find yourself without a clear picture of what a healthy, satisfying relationship looks like. With high divorce rates and widespread relationship dissatisfaction, it's rare to be surrounded by shining examples of loving, healthy partnerships.

The Changing Landscape of Relationships

In her book, *The Unhooked Generation*, Jillian Straus identifies "The Seven Evil Influences" that have shaped modern relationship challenges:

1. The Cult of I
2. Multiple Choice Culture
3. The Divorce Effect
4. The Inadvertent Effects of Feminism
5. The "Why Suffer?" Mentality
6. The Celebrity Standard
7. The Fallout from the Marriage Delay[48]

Straus argues that the core qualities needed for a committed, successful marriage often conflict with values prevalent in younger generations, as shown in the table below.[49] This misalignment can make it challenging to form lasting, satisfying relationships.

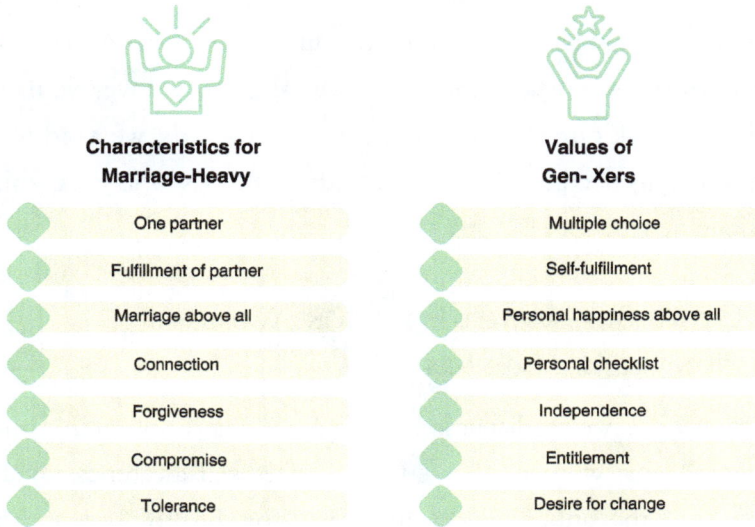

Characteristics for Marriage-Heavy	Values of Gen-Xers
One partner	Multiple choice
Fulfillment of partner	Self-fulfillment
Marriage above all	Personal happiness above all
Connection	Personal checklist
Forgiveness	Independence
Compromise	Entitlement
Tolerance	Desire for change

Figure 6. Characteristics for
Marriage-Heavy vs. Values of Gen-Xers

Straus's observations align with the work of renowned relationship researcher Dr. John Gottman, who identified compromise, tolerance, and forgiveness as essential components of successful marriages. The conclusion, which remains relevant today, is that the current generation's approaches to relationships are ineffective for building lasting connections.

Instead, Straus suggests, "In order for our generation to sustain true love, we need to accomplish a complete about-face. It turns out that finding true love is not an external process, but an internal one—it is not about finding a perfect match, but rather deciding to become someone who is both lovable and capable of being open, selfless, optimistic, brave, accepting, patient, and loving."[50]

This insight shifts the focus from finding the right partner to becoming the right partner. As Straus puts it, "Instead of demanding answers from potential partners, in order to get true love, we have to be willing to ask ourselves questions. In other words, we need to ask: Am I willing to become THE KIND OF PERSON who is capable of experiencing true love?"[51]

THE OTHER SIDE OF THE EQUATION: WOMEN'S RELATIONSHIP CHALLENGES

The challenges we've discussed throughout this book aren't unique to men. Many women also struggle with self-awareness, vulnerability, and the inner work necessary for healthy relationships. In her book, *Communion: The Female Search for Love*, author bell hooks points out that societal conditioning routinely leads women to believe they instinctively know how to give and receive love.[52] However, this assumption commonly proves false, as women, like men, struggle with the complexities of true intimacy.

Hooks observes that, "Women are often more interested in being loved than in the act of loving." This insight highlights a common obstacle to developing genuine partnerships—the focus on receiving love rather than actively loving.[53]

Now, this isn't about placing blame on women, men, or society at large. Rather, it's about recognizing the complex web of factors that influence our ability to form deep, meaningful connections. By understanding these broader influences, we can approach our relationship challenges with greater compassion and insight.

The real message here is that we all—as individuals and as a society—need to examine the roles we play in perpetuating these dynamics. Only by acknowledging this, can we begin to make conscious choices that lead to stronger relationships.

As a high performer, you are uniquely positioned to lead this change. By applying your drive and determination to personal growth and relationship skills, you can not only improve your own relationships, but also serve as a positive role model for others.

— — —

Vulnerability Unlocks Connection

Now that we've explored the internal and external dynamics that shape relationships, let's address one of the most powerful keys to deeper connections: vulnerability. Often misunderstood, especially among high performers, vulnerability is seen as weakness. However, true vulnerability is actually a sign of immense strength and the key to forging deeper bonds.

You're used to giving in ways that feel "safe"—at a distance, in short bursts, and without much emotional engagement. While you perceive this approach protects your heart, it limits the depth of your giving experience. This defense mechanism may serve you well in the boardroom but can leave you feeling isolated in your personal life.

Those who present the toughest exterior often carry the most sensitive hearts within. You may find that the "harsher" you are on the outside, the more sensitive you are on the inside. This disconnect between your external armor and internal tenderness makes vulnerability feel especially threatening.

The challenge with vulnerability is that it can feel like relinquishing control. Used to being in charge, calling the shots, and getting your way, you may fear that letting down your guard strips you of your power. But the paradox is that, in this presumed loss of control, you gain something far more valuable: the ability to engage authentically. Ultimately, you control your own story. That's why vulnerability is the greatest measure of courage—without it, you aren't fully seen, and not being seen limits your experience.

In the context of relationships, vulnerability is the soil in which intimacy grows. When you allow yourself to be vulnerable, you:

1. **Build trust**: By showing your whole self, flaws and all, you invite others to do the same.

2. **Deepen emotional connections**: Sharing your fears, hopes, and insecurities creates a deep bond that superficial interactions can't match.

3. **Enhance communication**: Being vulnerable allows for more, open, honest dialogue.

4. **Increase self-awareness**: Opening up helps you better understand yourself.

SELF-REFLECTION EXERCISE

Once you gain awareness of your own feelings and begin honoring them, the next step is sharing your emotional experience with others and, in turn, receiving theirs: "I see you, and I feel that you see me." Or, as Dr. Jill Bolte Taylor says, "When I let you see who I am, I empower you to do the same."[54]

To help you become more comfortable with vulnerability, try this powerful self-reflection exercise:

Stand in front of a mirror and look yourself in the eye. Keeping your gaze focused on yourself, answer the following prompts out loud:

- "I see…"
- "I hear…"
- "I feel…"
- "I worry…"
- "I know…"

This exercise allows you to express deeper truths and vulnerabilities in a safe way and explore the emotions doing so brings up for you. It's not about literal observations (like "I see my eyeballs"), but about deeper expressions of self.

For example:

- "I see a man who is scared."
- "I hear myself saying I'm going to die alone."
- "I feel tired of holding up this guard."
- "I worry I won't know how to go through this transformation."
- "I know I can do anything I set my mind to."

Though the exercise may sound simple, it has been remarkably challenging for many of my clients. The discomfort of literally facing themselves, along with the shame and hurt they feel, has caused some to stop or look away. This reaction is normal and expected. It's a sign that you're challenging your comfort zone, which is exactly where growth happens.

I encourage you to practice this exercise periodically. You may find that your reflections change over time, indicating personal growth and increased comfort with vulnerability.

The Ripple Effect of Vulnerability

As you become more comfortable with vulnerability in your personal life, you may find that it positively impacts other areas as well. Many of my clients report that embracing vulnerability has made them more empathetic leaders, better communicators in their professional lives, and more satisfied overall.

However, it's important to note that vulnerability doesn't mean oversharing or lacking boundaries. It's about being authentic and open in appropriate contexts. Learning to balance vulnerability with healthy boundaries is a vital skill in cultivating close relationships. As a high performer, you're likely adept at maintaining professional boundaries; apply this skill to your personal life by being open while still respecting your own and others' limits.

Embracing vulnerability is a journey, not a destination. There will be moments of discomfort and perhaps even setbacks. Showing up with vulnerability has no guarantees. But each time you choose to be vulnerable, you're building your capacity to love and live more fully.

Building on this, one of the most essential aspects of fostering deeper connections is recognizing how we communicate. We will now take a deeper look at understanding what that involves.

— — —

Communication Basics

Every time we communicate with another person, a complex process unfolds. Understanding how this works can significantly enhance your communication skills and, by extension, your emotional intelligence. Let's break it down.

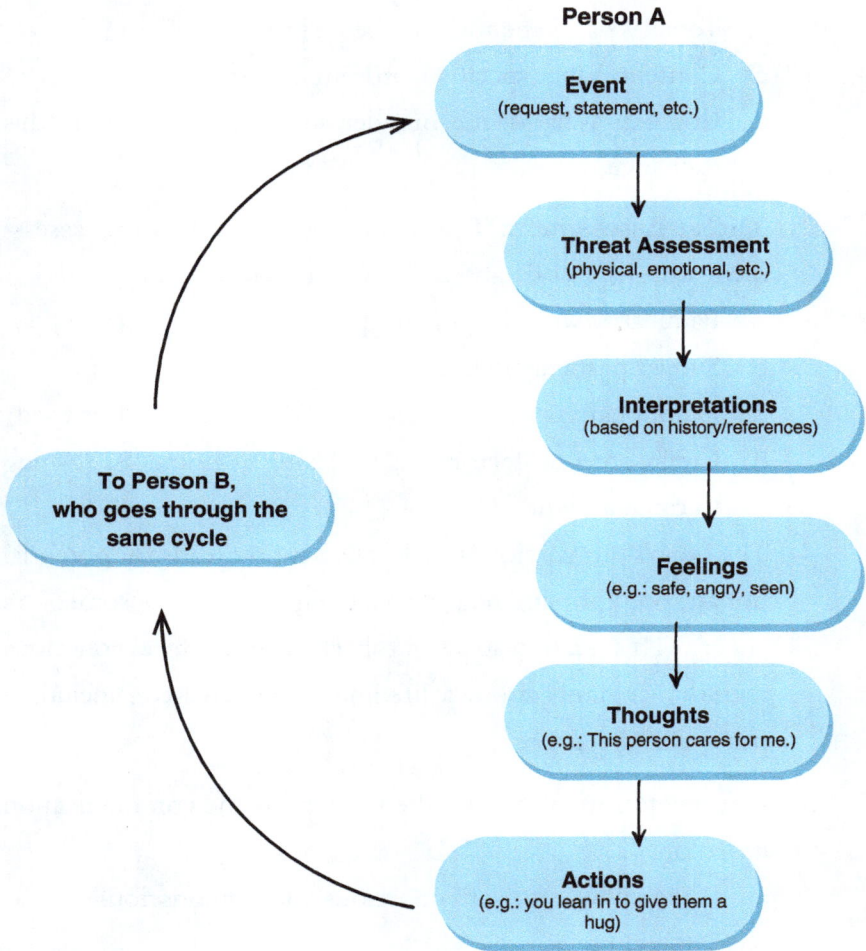

Person A

Event
(request, statement, etc.)

Threat Assessment
(physical, emotional, etc.)

Interpretations
(based on history/references)

To Person B,
who goes through the
same cycle

Feelings
(e.g.: safe, angry, seen)

Thoughts
(e.g.: This person cares for me.)

Actions
(e.g.: you lean in to give them a
hug)

Figure 7. Communication Flow Chart

THE COMMUNICATION PROCESS:

1. **The Event**: This is the initial communication, such as a request, statement, or question. In this scenario, Person A is the recipient of communication from Person B. Upon receiving the message, Person A's brain immediately evaluates:

    a. Clarity: How clear is the communication?
    b. Tone: What is the tone of the delivery?
    c. Content: What specific words are being used?
    d. Context: What is the broader situation surrounding this exchange?

2. **Threat Assessment**: The brain cross-references this assessment with its vast database of experiences, including:

    a. Familiarity with the person speaking
    b. Similar past experiences
    c. Emotional associations (e.g., with the tone or words used)
    d. Environmental factors (e.g., relaxing at home vs. rushing to catch a flight)

    The brain's primary job is survival, so it first scans for potential threats, both physical (e.g., fire) and emotional (e.g., someone's anger). This scan reaches far back, even before conscious memory. It draws from a lifetime of experiences, including pre-verbal memories.

3. **Interpretation**: The brain then interprets the communication based on:

    a. Personal beliefs (both conscious and subconscious)
    b. Preferences
    c. Past experiences
    d. Personal references (e.g., cultural background)

e. Current physical and emotional state (e.g., sleep quality, physical health, hunger, stress, and mood)

This generates a prediction about what might happen next, with the brain filling in whatever blanks it needs to in order to make its best guess.

4. **Feelings**: Next, the brain generates feelings about the situation based on those interpretations.

5. **Thoughts**: Those feelings lead to thoughts as you are putting together your analysis and what this all means to you.

6. **Actions**: The compilation of the steps above ultimately leads to the actions you take. Here, your values play a significant role, guiding you toward decisions that align with what matters most to you.

7. **Cycle Continuation**: Person A's response becomes the new "event" for Person B, and it all repeats, continuing the communication loop.

This cycle continues as long as the scenario is playing out.

Key Insights:

1. Perceived threats weigh heavily in decision-making.
2. Your first reaction may not always be accurate—ask yourself, "What else is in my universe?"
3. Many elements of communication are within your control.
4. Your brain makes educated guesses based on sensory input and past experiences.
5. Self-awareness and emotional attunement help you stay present and engaged in the moment.

6. Expanding your emotional vocabulary allows you to better understand and express your feelings. Emotional states differ widely between individuals, influenced by factors like age, culture, and life experiences.

7. Tuning into your body's signals can provide valuable information about your emotional state.

8. Your personal history shapes your interpretations and communication patterns.

9. Your brain has no direct access to the outside world, so its entire interpretation is based on internal processing.

10. Sometimes, putting words to your emotions can feel overwhelming, and focusing on the language to express the sensations in your body can be a more comfortable (and extremely valuable) place to start.

EXAMPLE SCENARIO: ADAM AND ALANA

Let's explore an example in the following scenario between Adam and his girlfriend, Alana.

- **Person A: Adam**
  - ○ **Event:** Alana excitedly tells him about an elaborate birthday party she's planning for her sister.
  - ○ **Assessment:** Adam is clear about the conversation. Alana's tone is excited, and she's sharing something meaningful to her.
  - ○ **Threat Assessment:** As the conversation continues, Adam's brain identifies a threat: he feels neglected and jealous of the attention Alana is giving her sister.

- **Interpretation:** Adam interprets Alana's excitement as a sign that she cares more about her sister than him.
- **Feeling:** This triggers feelings of rejection, insecurity, and frustration. Adam's shoulders tense, and his heart races.
- **Thought:** Adam thinks, "I don't need her. I don't want to hear this."
- **Action:** He lashes out, snapping at Alana.

- **Person B: Alana**
  - **Event:** Adam snaps at Alana.
  - **Assessment:** Alana understands Adam's words, but his tone is harsh and upset.
  - **Threat Assessment:** Alana's brain registers Adam's anger, making her feel emotionally fearful.
  - **Interpretation:** Alana interprets Adam's reaction as selfish and uncaring.
  - **Feeling:** She feels hurt and unsafe. Her body responds with shakiness and a racing heart.
  - **Thought:** Alana thinks, "He can never be happy for me. He's always angry."
  - **Action:** Alana walks away.

In this scenario, both Adam and Alana's responses are guided by their past experiences, current emotional states, and interpretations of the situation. This process, which happens in a fraction of a second, often operates outside of conscious awareness. They allow automatic reactions to control the conversation, missing the opportunity to connect. Instead, they could have:

- Paused to ask, "What else is in my universe?"

- Slowed down to gain control over their reactions
- Recognized the deeper triggers influencing their responses
- Tuned into their bodies for physical signals that something was off before reacting

By growing in self-awareness and emotional attunement, both parties could have altered the outcome.

***

Building meaningful relationships as a high performer requires more than just applying the same strategies that brought you professional success. It demands courage to examine your patterns, willingness to embrace vulnerability, and patience to develop new emotional skills. While the journey may feel challenging, remember that your capacity for growth and achievement can be channeled into creating deeper connections. By understanding and applying the principles we've explored—from the LAB Triangle to conscious communication—you can begin transforming your relationship patterns and experiencing the profound fulfillment that comes from authentic connection.

Reflection Questions

1. Which aspect of the LAB Triangle (Love, Agency, Boundary) may feel most challenging for you in relationships? Why?
2. How has being highly self-reliant impacted your close relationships? What are the pros and cons?
3. When do you tend to push people away in relationships? What situations typically trigger this response?

4. Think about a recent miscommunication in a relationship. How did your past experiences influence how you interpreted the situation?

5. What's one step you could take to be more vulnerable in your relationships?

CHAPTER NINE

BUILDING HEALTHY INTIMACY

In the previous chapter, we delved into the complexities of relationships and relationship dynamics. Now, we'll focus on practical ways to build and nurture meaningful connections. This chapter offers strategies and frameworks to help you develop committed relationships that endure the test of time.

We'll explore new concepts such as the L.O.V.E. framework and "Google Searching". We'll address intimacy and sexuality, helping you bridge emotional gaps that may have compromised your past relationships. Additionally, we'll look at balancing freedom and commitment—a common challenge for high performers—so you can find harmony between the two.

By the end of this chapter, you'll have practical tools for creating and sustaining fulfilling relationships that complement both your personal and professional life. These insights will deepen your understanding of yourself and enhance your connections with others.

— — —

Strategies for Cultivating Committed Relationships

Nurturing a committed, lasting relationship requires conscious effort and thoughtful intention. It's easy to fall into patterns that prioritize short-term comfort or self-preservation, but to create a truly satisfying partnership, you must be willing to invest greater effort.

Here are some approaches to help you navigate the challenges of intimacy while honoring your high-performance mindset:

1. **Clarify Your Intentions**: Verbalize your commitment. When you declare your intentions, they become more tangible and significant, aligning your actions with your goals. Understanding your motivations deepens your commitment.

2. **Mindful Social Connections**: Be conscious of the people you surround yourself with, both in person and through various media. Social contagion plays a significant role in your lifestyle choices, from sleep to spending habits. Seek out individuals whose approach to relationships and commitment inspires your personal growth.

3. **Operate From a "we" vs. "me" Mindset**: Shifting to a "we" mindset, rather than focusing on short-term impulses like running away, lying, or shutting down, fosters long-term, intentional decisions that strengthen your relationship. It's about turning toward your partner instead of turning away, being open about your needs, and practicing ongoing self-care. A "we" approach to love, rooted in self-love, promotes mutual joy, respect, accountability, and shared responsibility for each other's emotional welfare. It encourages honest communication and collaborative problem-solving, helping break cycles

of destructive behaviors. Mistakes become opportunities for growth, and trust deepens as partners work together, not against each other.

4. **Put In Intentional Effort**: Approach your relationship with the same determination you apply to other pursuits. This involves consistency, dedicated effort, clear communication, and deliberate actions. As Carl Jung said, "You are what you do, not what you say you'll do."

5. **Practice Patience and Self-Compassion**: Building a strong relationship takes time. Be patient with the process and practice self-compassion rather than harsh self-judgment.

6. **Reframe Your Perspective**: Challenge your existing definitions and associations. You determine the meaning that you attribute to things in life. If you've always seen commitment as a bad thing, try looking at how it could benefit you instead. Approach your feelings with curiosity instead of certainty. The next time you are faced with a triggering situation, try what I call "Google Searching." Pause and ask yourself:
   a. What else could be going on here?
   b. Am I misunderstanding this?
   c. How might I see this differently if I were feeling another emotion?

This "internal search engine," allows you to consider alternatives and helps you avoid jumping to conclusions. For example, imagine you come home, greet your partner with a, "Hey babe," a kiss, and a tap on the butt, but she doesn't respond as warmly as you'd hoped, which triggers your sense of rejection. You might instantly think, "Oh great, she's in a bad mood," and start pulling away. But what if you considered other possibilities? Maybe she was just distracted or busy. By staying curious and open, you could avoid unnecessary conflict and misunderstandings.

7. **Focus on Common Ground**: Identify shared goals and motivations with your partner. This helps lower defenses and redirects energy towards your shared vision.

8. **Use Positive Reinforcement**: Emphasize positive strategies over warnings or threats. Celebrate progress and reward positive behavior. Regularly acknowledge what's working well in your relationship.

9. **Embrace Imperfection**: Moments of disharmony don't necessarily indicate a broken relationship. Approach challenges with grace and compassion, understanding that mistakes are part of the journey.

10. **Model Desired Behaviors**: Demonstrate the behaviors you wish to see in your relationship.

11. **Develop Self-Soothing Techniques**: Learn to manage your triggers through practices like deep breathing, journaling, connecting with support systems, spending time in nature, exercising, or listening to music.

12. **Know Each Other's Love Languages**: Identifying and meeting each other's love language needs is key to relationship fulfillment. You can research more about love languages or read *The Five Love Languages* by Gary Chapman.

13. **Make Understanding One Another Your Goal (Not Being Right):** Safety is no longer about perfection or controlling your emotions and environment. Communication becomes about understanding, not defending. As Dr. Neil Clark Warren says, "If you know that your partner has understood your thoughts and feelings, you will maintain a closeness even if you continue to disagree on the issue in point."[55]

14. **Practice Effective Communication:**
    a. Be mindful of your language, recognizing that it typically takes five positive interactions to counteract one negative one.[56]
    b. When triggered, take a holistic inventory of your state, including physical state and stress levels.
    c. Be concise in conversations, especially during emotional discussions.
    d. Know when to request a time-out, ensuring you revisit the conversation when you're better equipped to engage fully.
    e. Don't overwhelm each other in a conversation. You might prefer direct, to-the-point communication, but this can be difficult for people to do in emotional conversations.
    f. As a high performer, be aware of your tendency to over-analyze or "outthink" your partner. Remember, your partner is not an opponent to conquer. As Lao Tzu wisely said, "He who conquers others is strong; he who conquers himself is mighty."

— — —

The L.O.V.E. Framework for Lasting Partnerships

Next, let's explore the L.O.V.E. framework. The L.O.V.E. framework offers clear, actionable steps to strengthen your relationship by cultivating mutual respect, understanding, and commitment.

L: LOVE

Love, in its truest form, is found in the deep end. Love is a verb. It's not just a feeling, but a series of actions and choices you make every day. It involves:

- Being truthful, even when it's hard
- Paying attention to both small and big things
- Choosing to act with care, respect, and kindness
- Creating safety and trust through loyalty, responsibility, accountability, and commitment

Love is about making a choice every day to stick with someone, even (and especially) when it's tough. It's promising to be there for them, no matter what. The thing is that many of us misunderstand love. We think that simply respecting or trusting someone means we love them, or we seek a partner without truly understanding love itself.

There are countless books about love, yet many people still struggle to experience real, earnest love in their lives. It's akin to aspiring to be a successful entrepreneur but avoiding the hard work to get there. Similarly, people want love, but they aren't always ready to put in the effort it requires. Love isn't some mystical concept reserved for the fortunate few. It's available to everyone, but it takes discipline.

O: OPPORTUNITY

This is about actively seeking ways to strengthen your relationship. It includes:

- **Gratitude**: Appreciating someone goes a long way in allowing them to feel seen and showing that you took the time to notice their actions. Gratitude also creates a positive reinforcement of what behaviors should be repeated. Regularly express appreciation for your partner and the things they do.

- **Generosity**: Generosity is not about being generous with your wealth, but rather with your forgiveness, time, attention, and care. It's about creating space for healthy individuation, listening, considering your partner, and giving them the benefit of the doubt instead of jumping to conclusions.

- **Safety**: I cannot emphasize enough the importance of this one. Recall that your brain's primary job is survival, and when the safety in a relationship is threatened, it acts like a poison that undermines the foundation, making it difficult to recover a sense of safety. When you open up to someone and share the deepest parts of yourself, only to have that used against you in an argument, when you trust someone to hold what's sacred to you and feel betrayed, or when you breach the boundaries of your relationship through infidelity, the resulting hurdle is difficult enough for others let alone for you, with your already impenetrable walls. Create an emotionally safe environment where both you and your partner can be vulnerable.

- **Experiences**: Your brain craves novelty, so rather than letting your relationship get stuck in a rut, continue to seek out new experiences to share together. They don't have to be grand—

even a hike in a new location or dining at a new restaurant can suffice. Perhaps you both explore new opportunities for sexual intimacy (new places, positions, or ways to connect without sex). Share the responsibility of coming up with ideas, rather than leaving it to just one person. Having new experiences planned also gives you both something to look forward to.

V: Vision

Create a shared vision for your relationship. This involves:

- Discussing how you want to show up and what kind of partners you want to be
- Discussing what kind of partners you want to have
- Setting individual and collective goals (e.g., discussing fitness goals, places you want to travel to)
- Aligning on your definitions of significant concepts like support and partnership
- Planning for your future together (e.g., when you want to retire and how you want to spend the rest of your life)

E: Empathy

Empathy is a gift that benefits both the giver and the receiver. As you grow in self-awareness and become more attuned to your own emotions, your ability to recognize and understand other people's emotions increases, and you become more fluent in the language of feelings. This greater attunement allows you to sense what others are experiencing. The information you receive from their emotions affects your own feelings, and you can use this insight to regulate your responses. As Rick Hanson says, "Empathy contains an inherent generosity: you give the willingness to be moved by another person."[57]

Empathy is crucial for understanding and connection. It involves:

- Trying to understand your partner's perspectives
- Acknowledging and validating their feelings
- Using your understanding to inform your actions and reactions

To truly understand someone's feelings and actions, you must consider how they interpreted a situation, not how you would interpret it, or even how you think they should interpret it if you were in their shoes.

Conflict is inevitable, but empathy allows you to approach it selflessly, seeking first to understand rather than to be understood. When combined with respect, empathy can reshape harmful conflict into helpful learning and create space to realize that your differences may stem from varying perspectives rather than from being fundamentally different people. Often, we fail to recognize how much of our interpretation of a situation is our own construction rather than an objective reality.

L.O.V.E.! Yes, it can be difficult to do. No, I'm not saying it's easy. But by consistently applying this L.O.V.E. framework, you can create a strong foundation for a lasting, fulfilling partnership. The key is to keep at it while maintaining open dialogue with your partner and reserving judgment. This allows you to give each other grace: you're not perfect, you're going to get it wrong, but you're going to keep trying (with an honest self-assessment of how diligent your effort is).

— — —

Bridging the Sexual-Emotional Gap

Intimacy and sexuality can be complex areas, especially for high performers. You are used to succeeding in other areas of life, but the deep emotional connection that underlies true intimacy often feels hard to reach.

Sexual energy is an incredibly intense and powerful force that demands our attention and understanding. The line between love and sex often blurs, creating confusion where you might mistake sexual connection for love. However, in a healthy relationship, there is a stark difference between the energy created by sex and the energy created by love-making. Sex generates less control, operating primarily through physical and biological drives. In contrast, when love mixes with sex, it elicits a more calm and centering energy that you can use constructively. This love-infused intimacy initiates more in your spirit than your body. If you tune in carefully, you can feel the different vibrations they each create inside you. There is also an important distinction between love and desire: while love is comprehensive and deep-rooted, desire tends to be driven primarily by sexual factors. Understanding the difference is an advantage in developing a healthy, committed relationship.

Understanding Your Sexual Paradigm

Your approach to sex and intimacy is greatly influenced by your past experiences and beliefs. To gain insight into your sexual paradigm, consider these questions:

- Were you parentified at a young age?
- Did you take on the role of protecting a parent?
- Do you believe that love and erotic expression are incompatible with the same person?

- Do your beliefs about being a selfish lover or trusting intimacy stem from early observations?
- Did you observe your primary caregivers express affection with ease?

These questions shed light on how you relate to intimacy today. Understanding your sexual paradigm can help you identify patterns and beliefs that may be hindering your ability to form deep, intimate connections.

THE PERFORMANCE TRAP

For many high performers, sexual performance takes on heightened importance. It becomes a way to feel something, to express yourself, especially when emotional or verbal expression seems difficult. Sex becomes a safe space where you can admit your desire for connection—though you may convince yourself afterward that you can leave that truth behind once the act is over.

You come to sex seeking what you imagine love would feel like, even if just for a brief moment. You hope to feel close, connected, and intimate. However, when sex falls short of this deeper connection, your longing remains, which drives you to pursue more sex, hoping next time will be different. The stronger your desire to feel seen and loved, the more obsessive your pursuit of sex becomes—you keep believing it might soothe the pain of the emotional void.

This also fuels your frustration, as it feels like a partner has power over you by either offering or withholding sex. Yet they typically have no idea how intensely sex is tied to your emotional needs because, more often than not, neither do you.

INTEGRATING EMOTIONAL AND PHYSICAL INTIMACY

To bridge the gap between emotional and physical intimacy:

1. Recognize the emotional needs underlying your sexual desires. What are you really seeking through sexual encounters?
2. Practice vulnerability in your sexual encounters. Allow yourself to be seen, not just physically, but also emotionally.
3. Communicate openly about your needs and desires. This includes both sexual preferences and emotional needs.
4. Work on expressing emotions verbally as well as physically. Develop your emotional vocabulary and practice using it.
5. Understand that true intimacy involves being fully seen and accepted. This includes your strengths, weaknesses, fears, and desires.

In this work, especially at first and possibly for a long time, you may struggle to verbally express your emotions. It requires developing the skill of intimate expression through language, which is not something men are often socialized to do. Control is important to you, and you're uncomfortable with things you don't do well. Emotional expression, particularly verbal, feels unsafe and leaves you feeling out of control.

However, what you express through physical and sexual intimacy is just as important as what your partner conveys through words. Both of you have a responsibility to learn each other's emotional languages. Your partner should develop an understanding of your form of sensual bonding, just as you need to engage with their verbal expression.

One of the greatest fears about love and intimacy is that there's no place to hide. Yet there's freedom in being fully seen. As John Welwood says, "When we reveal ourselves to our partner and find that this brings healing rather than harm, we make an important discovery—that intimate relationships can provide a sanctuary from the world of façades, a sacred space where we can be ourselves, as we are ... This kind of unmasking—speaking our truth, sharing our inner struggles, and revealing our raw edges—is sacred activity, which allows two souls to meet and touch more deeply."[58]

— — —

Navigating Emotional Growth In Relationships

As you move toward emotional growth and deeper intimacy, you're likely to experience several changes. Understanding these potential shifts can help you navigate them more effectively.

You'll Consider Your Role In Relationship Dynamics

Instead of defensively thinking, "Women will hurt you, so be careful," you'll start asking yourself more constructive questions: "How am I contributing to her reactions? Why am I pushing her away? What fears am I harboring? How can I open up and engage more fully?"

This new perspective isn't about learning a foreign language of love, but rather rediscovering one you've always known. When you embrace these questions and take responsibility for your part in relationships, you'll find yourself becoming more fluent in expressing and receiving love. You'll connect more deeply with others as your authentic self emerges, no longer hidden behind a mask of fear. This shift frees you from needing to justify past decisions made to protect your ego, creating space for more genuine, fulfilling connections.

You'll Notice the Inefficiencies of Your Ego

As you begin to create new definitions of what it means to get close to someone, allow your walls to come down, and trust that intimacy no longer needs to be overridden with fear, you also begin to see the inefficiencies of your ego. You learn that as long as you are holding onto your past, it is holding onto you, and emotions time travel you back to relive your history.

Authors Katherine Ludwig and Edward Hess share, "To quiet our ego is to perceive others and the world without filtering everything through a self-focused lens and to tamp down on negative or self-protective 'inner talk' that is driven consciously or subconsciously by our fears and insecurities."[59]

This is not about "killing your ego." Instead, I encourage you to "hold your ego"—not suppress it, but embrace it, thank it, and honor its service to you. Then, gently reaffirm that it's not needed in this space. Let your ego become a servant to your mind, and your mind a servant to your heart, for while the ego can be a good servant, it is not a good master.

Existing Relationships Might Get Rockier

Challenges in a relationship are not an automatic indication that it's time for someone new. Rather, perhaps it's simply time to try something new within the existing relationship. However, trying to be your best for the wrong person can bring out the worst in you and make you shut down even further.

As you grow and change, your existing relationships may experience turbulence. This is normal and even necessary. It's important to communicate openly with your partner about the changes you're experiencing and invite her to join you on this journey of growth.

Your Ideal Partner May Change

As you move toward personal growth, you may notice a shift in what you look for in an intimate partner. You're likely to move beyond surface-level relationships, seeking more profound emotional bonds. You might find yourself longing for a partner who embodies a stronger feminine presence—someone with an open, compassionate heart, who offers unconditional acceptance, has the strength to support you through challenges, and the firmness to hold you accountable, while standing by you consistently.

Your ideal partner may need to play various roles as you grow. At times, she might nurture you like an infant when you're feeling vulnerable, parent you like an adolescent when you are navigating new emotional territories, and love you as an equal adult. This multifaceted support requires both partners to strengthen their own capacity—to hold space for each other's emotional needs, provide safety spiritually, sexually, and socially, and maintain a strong sense of self and boundaries. This journey prepares you for such a balanced, mature partnership.

People You Love Might Not Change

Unfortunately, change is not something you can force on someone. So, what do you do if you find yourself growing in a relationship with a partner who is resistant to growing themselves? You have two main options:

1. Choose to accept them as they are, hoping that by continuing to model more conscious behavior, someday, they will choose to pursue their own growth journey.

2. Decide that you are both better served apart than together, which sometimes is the difficult reality.

This can elicit feelings of grief—you may need to decide which relationships are worth keeping and which ones you may need to let go of. Keep in mind, it's okay to outgrow relationships that no longer serve your highest good.

— — —

The Path to Secure Attachment

As you navigate these relationship changes, let's explore more deeply how secure attachment can develop through healthy relationships. The beauty of secure attachment lies in its potential for growth. Even if only one partner has a secure attachment style, their presence can nurture the other to develop it through sensitivity and encouragement. Think of it like learning a new language: while it might feel awkward and uncomfortable at first, with consistent practice and the right environment, you can become fluent in the language of secure connection.

It's important to note that a secure attachment doesn't necessarily stem from a trouble-free, warm, and caring upbringing. Like your own story, it's multi-dimensional, influenced by family, genetics, and a whole portfolio of life experiences. Some people develop secure attachment through positive events in adulthood, such as loving relationships that change their beliefs about love and intimacy. Others achieve it through the willingness to do the difficult work of healing childhood voids and creating new ways of being.

The journey toward secure attachment often involves:

- Recognizing that past coping mechanisms, while they served you well before, may now be limiting your capacity for connection
- Allowing yourself to be gradually more vulnerable with trusted partners
- Learning to communicate your needs clearly instead of expecting others to guess them
- Developing comfort with both giving and receiving emotional support
- Building tolerance for the natural ebbs and flows of relationships

Consider tracking your progress through these markers of developing secure attachment:

- Increased comfort with emotional expression
- Greater ability to seek support when needed
- More consistent communication during conflict
- Reduced anxiety about abandonment or engulfment
- Growing trust in your partner's availability
- Better balance between independence and intimacy

The key takeaway is this: your beliefs, attachment styles, and approaches to vulnerability and intimacy can change. And the power to change them rests with you. Just as you've mastered other complex skills in your life, you can develop the capacity for secure attachment through conscious effort and practice.

This potential for transformation in how we connect with others naturally leads us to one of the most challenging paradoxes in relationships—how to balance our need for freedom with our desire for commitment.

— — —

Balancing Freedom and Commitment

As you experience shifts in how you view relationships and intimacy, one of the most challenging aspects is reconciling the need for both freedom and commitment, which often feel like opposing forces. For many high performers, especially those with avoidant attachment styles, the fear of entrapment in relationships can feel overwhelming. But a relationship where you feel close and safe doesn't have to stifle your sense of freedom or adventure. In fact, you can create a balance where passion and excitement continue to thrive as intimacy deepens.

It's about seeing love through a new lens, one in which the element of mystery between you and your beloved can fuel your curiosity and interest rather than trigger your fear and insecurity. Love in this way allows you to feel seen for who you are and also transcend who you have been. Over and over, it is sending the message, "I choose you," to one another, and seeing the ways in which you serve each other and the things you may give up as an honor, not a sacrifice.

This kind of intimacy requires certain ingredients to thrive:

1. Connection rooted in trust
2. Self-awareness to know your landmines and triggers
3. A heart-centered approach that places great importance on empathy

Here, intimacy isn't just about sex, and talking isn't the only way to build this foundation. It includes sharing experiences, doing things together, laughter, compliments, support, touch (holding hands, massage, embrace), love letters, small gestures like making their morning coffee, exercising together, connecting to what you love about each other, gratitude, forgiveness, letting go of the small stuff, spending time apart, respect—ALWAYS, and self-love.

Being close to someone does not need to mean losing yourself. On the contrary, maintaining your individuality supports the building of healthier intimate bonds. When you and your partner no longer need to equate the false sense of control you feel from the predictability and "known-ness" of one another as the only way to feel safe in the relationship, and you are able to trust one another, it sweetens the journey of exploring the mystery of each other.

As Esther Perel says in her book, *Mating in Captivity*, "Erotic intelligence is about creating distance, then bringing that space to life."[60] She goes on to say, "What makes sustaining desire over time so difficult is that it requires reconciling two opposing forces: freedom and commitment."[61] Freedom and autonomy allow you and your partner to maintain your individuality, which creates space for you both to show up to the commitment as your whole self and because you chose to, with an energy that enlivens the space and continues to draw you in by feeding this cycle.

Commitment brings significant psychological benefits. Though keeping options open can seem appealing and has its advantages, failing to commit also has psychological costs. Although commitment—especially in marriage—might seem restrictive or even be referred to as a "ball and chain," it can actually bring a sense of relief and ease. Making a commitment often reduces inner conflict, leaving you feeling more at peace. In fact, people frequently describe the experience of a good commitment as "a weight off my shoulders" or "feeling lighter," showing just how freeing commitment can feel.

***

It's not uncommon for my clients to start this journey thinking it's ridiculous, but end up feeling its real impact. Love and compassion can grow your heart, as you realize that the walls protecting you were also blocking you from experiencing the depth of connection you truly desire. In fact, the same brain circuits that are responsible for establishing a bond between parents and children are repurposed for romantic relationships.

In redefining partnership, intimacy, love, and vulnerability, you create more room for your relationships to grow. You work your shit out WITH each other, instead of ON each other. When either of you makes a mistake, it isn't labeled as a reflection of your internal essence. By replacing fear with courage, you can make choices based on the present, not the past. In facing your emotions, no longer do they live in the shadow and become a playground for the darkness that exists in you. Instead of reacting with defensiveness or pretending not to care, you can acknowledge your true feelings. This shift allows you to invest energy in building healthy connections rather than wasting energy on repairing and recovering from every episode where you withheld yourself.

Cultivating deep personal relationships is a journey, not a destination. It requires ongoing effort, patience, and a willingness to grow and change.

Remember:

- Communication is key. Strive to understand and be understood.
- Vulnerability is strength, not weakness.
- Trust and intimacy are built over time through consistent actions.
- Authenticity allows for true connection.
- Love is a verb—it requires action and choice.

Be patient with yourself on this journey of learning new skills and rewiring old patterns. It won't always be easy, but the rewards are immeasurable. Your capacity for love and connection is vast, and by applying the principles in this chapter, you can unlock this potential to create relationships that not only support your success but enrich your life in ways you may never have imagined. Keep in mind that the goal isn't perfection, but progress. Every step toward more open, true, and loving relationships brings you closer to a more fulfilling life.

Reflection Questions

Consider an important relationship in your life as you answer these questions:

1. In what ways does this relationship challenge you to grow?

2. How effectively do you communicate your needs in this relationship?
3. How do you typically handle conflicts in this relationship?
4. Does this relationship bring a sense of peace to your life?

Reflect on these questions periodically to track your growth and identify areas for improvement in your relationships.

Conclusion

Your Future Awaits

Here we are. While this book may be coming to a close, your real work is just beginning. In my younger years, I took pride in never shedding a tear. I thought I was tough. I would never have guessed that, years later, I'd write a book about living from the heart. Yet here I am, and my heart lives in every sentence on these pages.

My hope is that through these words, you've felt seen for the beauty within you, encouraged to heal what still hurts, and inspired to amend any harm you have caused others. Most importantly, I hope you now stand more fully in the greatness that has always been yours.

Take a moment to acknowledge how far you've come. You've faced the unique challenges of being a high performer in a complex world, delving deep into the emotions and beliefs that shape your life. You now hold the tools to rewire your brain, cultivate healthier relationships, and align your decisions with your core values.

This work isn't for the faint of heart. It takes real courage to face the parts of yourself you've long kept hidden, to lean into vulnerability, and to step outside your comfort zone. But as you've discovered, true strength comes from accepting your whole self—flaws, fears, and all. The payoff is extraordinary: not just becoming a better leader but becoming a more authentic, grounded human being.

This process isn't about perfection. It's about integration—bringing together the driven achiever, the vulnerable soul, the caring partner—into a more cohesive whole. The road ahead won't always be smooth. Old habits may resurface, and growth might feel uncomfortable. But that's part of evolving. What matters is how you respond. Will you meet challenges with curiosity and patience or frustration and self-criticism? Mistakes are inevitable, but they are also invaluable opportunities to learn and refine your approach.

As you move forward, consider the legacy you want to leave behind. How do you want to be remembered? What you do with your gifts matters more than the gifts themselves. Your impact will be determined by what you feel deeply connected to—whether that's family, community, spirit, or purpose. Each time you show up as your authentic self, you inspire others to do the same. Your vulnerability gives others permission to remove their own masks. By prioritizing your emotional well-being, you're planting the seeds for deeper connections rooted in empathy and compassion.

At the beginning of this book, I said the world needs you, and I believe that more than ever. But even more important is the fact that *you deserve this*. You deserve to live in peace, love, and safety. You didn't ask to be born with this calling, but trust that a higher purpose breathed it into you. And that calling requires all of you—not just your brilliant mind but also your tender heart. As Rumi reminds us, "You are the Soul of the Soul of the Universe, and your name is Love." Your task is not to seek for love but to return to the truth of who you are. When you do, your light will shine unmistakably.

The future may be unpredictable, you're more than ready for whatever comes next. Keep exploring your inner world with curiosity.

Meet challenges with a growth mindset. Surround yourself with people who support and challenge you to reach your highest potential. And above all, never lose sight of the immense capacity for love, connection, and impact that resides within you.

This is your moment to step into a new level of greatness. Keep leaning in, keep stretching, and keep giving. On the other side of this work lies a version of yourself—and a life—more meaningful than you can yet imagine.

Here's to your continued growth, your expanding influence, and the extraordinary future that awaits you. The adventure is just beginning, and I couldn't be more excited to see where it takes you.

Additional Resources for Continued Growth

To support your ongoing journey, consider exploring these resources:

Recommended Books:
- *Mindsight: The New Science of Personal Transformation* by Dan Siegel
- *The Untethered Soul: The Journey Beyond Yourself* by Michael Singer
- *Think Again: The Power of Knowing What You Don't Know* by Adam Grant
- *Rising Strong: How the Ability to Reset Transforms the Way We Live, Love, Parent, and Lead* by Brené Brown
- *Mating in Captivity: Unlocking Erotic Intelligence* by Esther Perel
- *The Male Brain: A Breakthrough Understanding of How Men and Boys Think* by Louann Brizendine
- *Thinking, Fast and Slow* by Daniel Kahneman

Other Tools for Holistic Well-being:
- Regular exercise
- Healthy diet
- Adequate sleep
- Limiting alcohol and drug use
- Regular health check-ups
- Morning routine for grounding
- Exploring spirituality or mindfulness practices

Acknowledgments

I did not write this book alone. It is the work of the many teachers I've had along the way—the friends, therapists, healers, mentors, and mentees who allowed us to share space. The experts who have shared their wisdom through books, podcasts, and classes I continue to learn from. To all of my high-performing clients who have honored me by sharing their sacred journeys and fed my passion for this work— your courage inspires me. To every draft-reader who generously spent time reading a version of this book and offering their input, thank you!

Marissa, my amazing editor ... you are such a gift and an incredible partner. Leb, Jennifer, Lisa ... thank you for being such supportive teammates! To everyone who ever made me doubt myself, told me, "no," and said something couldn't be done, thank you for fueling my fire. To Mother Nature, thank you for being my refuge. To my family, thank you for the ongoing support. Amoo Kavoos, your unwavering love and dependability never go unnoticed. Amoo Jalil, your light shines bright every day. Amit, thank you for creating the space to make this book possible and for your deep care. You are such an incredible soul, and I am forever grateful to you.

To my HQ (Ari, Maya, Hedi), the community you have given me has been truly priceless. I'm so grateful for the way you all rallied at the end—life savers! Ari, my angel, so much of this book exists because of you. Your love is priceless (infinity!). I am so grateful for what God has put into your heart. Dear Fawzia, your teachings are a welcome companion on an often lonely journey.

Xavier, you are a pivotal part of my journey. Thank you for all that you are, for challenging me, and for letting me pick your brain endlessly. The world needs you—let your light shine (and check the dryer!).

Mom and Dad, thank you for making me believe I could achieve anything and for giving me the space to be "different." Words can't express my love and gratitude. Dad, I cherish the ways in which I am the best of you. Mom, you are one of the smartest and most selfless people I have ever known. The world is not big enough to contain all that God put into your heart. I pray that between this world and the next, your life feels complete.

To God, I pray that when we meet, I have not made You regret the gifts you gave me. I am certain there are more names to add to this list; to anyone who feels overlooked, please know that your impact is felt and appreciated.

To Mohammad, you are the reason I exist as I do, and the best of me is because of you. Thank you for always making me feel like I was God's gift to the world. It is because of you that I care for and understand this population the way I do. My greatest prayer is that my work will honor your legacy and ensure your life was not in vain.

Works Cited

1. YourTango. (May 19, 2023). *The Ugliest Truth About Success Nobody Will Tell You*. YourTango. Retrieved May 19, 2023, from https://www.yourtango.com/self/ugliest-truth-about-success-nobodywill-tell-you

2. Grover, T. (2013). *Relentless: From Good to Great to Unstoppable*. Scribner. (p. 23).

3. Gerber, M. E. (1995). *The E-Myth Revisited: Why Most Small Businesses Don't Work and What to Do About It*. HarperCollins. (p. 24).

4. Siegel, D. J. (2010). *Mindsight: The New Science of Personal Transformation*. Bantam Books.

5. Cozolino, L. (2010). *The Neuroscience of Psychotherapy: Healing the Social Brain*. W. W. Norton & Company. (p. 309).

6. Cozolino, L. (2010). *The Neuroscience of Psychotherapy: Healing the Social Brain*. W. W. Norton & Company. (p. 9, p. 181).

7. Siegel, D. J. (2010). *Mindsight: The New Science of Personal Transformation*. Bantam Books. (p. xvii).

8. Siegel, D. J. (2010). *Mindsight: The New Science of Personal Transformation*. Bantam Books. (p. 166).

9. Cozolino, L. (2010). *The Neuroscience of Psychotherapy: Healing the Social Brain*. W. W. Norton & Company. (p. 222).

10. Satir, Virginia. *The New Peoplemaking*. Palo Alto, CA: Science and Behavior Books, 1988.

11. Kahneman, D. (2011). *Thinking, Fast and Slow*. Farrar, Straus and Giroux. (p. 87).

12. Tolle, E. (2003). *Stillness Speaks*. New World Library. (pp. 14-15).

13. "Attachment theory." In Encyclopedia Britannica. Retrieved from https://www.britannica.com/science/attachment-theory

14. "Attachment theory." In Encyclopedia Britannica. Retrieved from https://www.britannica.com/science/attachment-theory

15. Cozolino, L. (2010). *The Neuroscience of Psychotherapy: Healing the Social Brain*. W. W. Norton & Company. (p. 204).

16. Levine, A., & Heller, R. S. F. (2010). *Attached: The New Science of Adult Attachment and How It Can Help You Find - and Keep - Love*. TarcherPerigee. (pp. 12, 14)

17. Dalio, R. (2017). *Principles: Life and Work*. Simon & Schuster. (p. 206).

18. Cozolino, L. (2010). *The Neuroscience of Psychotherapy: Healing the Social Brain*. W. W. Norton & Company. (p. 118).

19. Cozolino, L. (2010). *The Neuroscience of Psychotherapy: Healing the Social Brain*. W. W. Norton & Company. (p. 122).

20. Cozolino, L. (2010). *The Neuroscience of Psychotherapy: Healing the Social Brain*. W. W. Norton & Company. (p. 81).

21. Coyle, D. (2018). *The Culture Code: The Secrets of Highly Successful Groups*. Bantam. (p. 25).

22. Goleman, D. (2006). *Social Intelligence: The New Science of Human Relationships*. Bantam. (p. 15).

23. Cozolino, L. (2010). *The Neuroscience of Psychotherapy: Healing the Social Brain*. W. W. Norton & Company. (p. 168).

24. Davidson, R. J., & Begley, S. (2012). *The Emotional Life of Your Brain: How Its Unique Patterns Affect the Way You Think, Feel, and Live—And How You Can Change Them*. Penguin Books. (p. 14).

25. Rucker, M. (2023, July 6). *The Delicate Dance of High-Arousal Enjoyment*. Psychology Today. Retrieved from https://www.psychologytoday.com/intl/blog/the-science-of-fun/202307/the-delicate-dance-of-high-arousal-enjoyment

26. Kahneman, D. (2011). *Thinking, Fast and Slow*. Farrar, Straus and Giroux.

27. Dalio, R. (2017). *Principles: Life and Work*. Simon & Schuster. (p. 236).

28. Goleman, D. (1995). *Emotional Intelligence: Why It Can Matter More Than IQ*. Bantam Books.

29. Brizendine, L. (2010). *The Male Brain*. Broadway Books. (p. 105).

30. Brizendine, L. (2010). *The Male Brain*. Broadway Books. (p. 127).

31. Sharot, T. (2017). *The Influential Mind: What the Brain Reveals About Our Power to Change Others* (p. 41). New York, NY: Henry Holt and Company.

32. Spiker, T. (2020). *The Only Leaders Worth Following: How to Build a Winning Culture* (p. 56). Aperio.

33. Pink, D. H. (2009). *Drive: The Surprising Truth About What Motivates Us*. Riverhead Books.

34. Pink, D. H. (2009). *Drive: The Surprising Truth About What Motivates Us*. Riverhead Books. (p. 131).

35. Hess, E., & Ludwig, K. (2017). *Humility Is the New Smart: Rethinking Human Excellence in the Smart Machine Age*. Berrett-Koehler Publishers. (p. 5).

36. Saban, Nick, and Adam C. Smith. *Saban: The Making of a Coach*. HarperCollins, 2015.

37. Robinson, B. E. (2020, April 26). *The 90-Second Rule Builds Self-Control*. Psychology Today. Retrieved from https://www.psychologytoday.com/ca/blog/the-right-mindset/202004/the-90-second-rule-builds-self-control

38. Shaw, George Bernard. *Maxims for Revolutionists*. 1903.

39. Hanson, R. (2009). *Buddha's Brain: The Practical Neuroscience of Happiness, Love, and Wisdom*. New Harbinger Publications. (p. 139).

40. Dyer, W. (2001). *The Power of Intention: Learning to Co-create Your World Your Way*. Hay House.

41. Levine, A., & Heller, R. S. F. (2010). *Attached: The New Science of Adult Attachment and How It Can Help You Find - and Keep - Love*. TarcherPerigee. (p. 166).

42. Cozolino, L. (2010). *The Neuroscience of Psychotherapy: Healing the Social Brain*. W. W. Norton & Company. (p. 194).

43. Cashman, K. (2008). *Leadership From the Inside Out: Becoming a Leader for Life*. San Francisco: Berrett-Koehler Publishers.

44. Grant, A. (2021). *Think Again: The Power of Knowing What You Don't Know*. Viking. (p. 92).

45. Levine, A., & Heller, R. S. F. (2010). *Attached: The New Science of Adult Attachment and How It Can Help You Find - and Keep - Love*. TarcherPerigee. (p. 119).

46. Vaillant, G. E. (2012). *Triumphs of Experience: The Men of the Harvard Grant Study*. Belknap Press of Harvard University Press.

47. Robbins, A. (1991). *Awaken the Giant Within: How to Take Immediate Control of Your Mental, Emotional, Physical and Financial Destiny!* Free Press. (p. 95).

48. Straus, J. (2006). *Unhooked Generation: The Truth About Why We're Still Single*. Hyperion. (pp. 2-28).

49. Straus, J. (2006). *Unhooked Generation: The Truth About Why We're Still Single*. Hyperion. (p. 166).

50. Straus, J. (2006). *Unhooked Generation: The Truth About Why We're Still Single*. Hyperion. (p. 207).

51. Straus, J. (2006). *Unhooked Generation: The Truth About Why We're Still Single*. Hyperion. (p. 241).

52. hooks, b. (2002). *Communion: The Female Search for Love*. HarperCollins.

53. hooks, b. (2002). *Communion: The Female Search for Love*. HarperCollins.

54. Bolte Taylor, J. (2022). *Whole Brain Living* (p. 139). Hay House LLC.

55. Warren, N. C., & Abraham, K. (2005). *Falling in Love for All the Right Reasons: How To Find Your Soul Mate*. Center Street. (p. 175).

56. Gottman JM. *The seven principles for making marriage work: A practical guide from the country's foremost relationship expert*. 1st ed. New York, NY: Three Rivers Press; 1999.

57. Hanson, R. (2009). *Buddha's Brain: The Practical Neuroscience of Happiness, Love, and Wisdom*. New Harbinger Publications. (p. 139).

58. Welwood, J. (1997). *Love and awakening: Discovering the sacred path of intimate relationship.* Shambhala.

59. Hess, E., & Ludwig, K. (2017). *Humility Is the New Smart: Rethinking Human Excellence in the Smart Machine Age.* Berrett-Koehler Publishers. (p. 79).

60. Perel, E. (2006). *Mating in Captivity: Unlocking Erotic Intelligence.* Harper. (p. 32).

61. Perel, E. (2006). *Mating in Captivity: Unlocking Erotic Intelligence.* Harper. (p. 82).

www.ingramcontent.com/pod-product-compliance
Lightning Source LLC
Chambersburg PA
CBHW071940090426
42740CB00011B/1759